The Holy Rosary through the Writings
of Saint Alphonsus de Liguori

The

Holy Rosary

Through the Writings of Saint Alphonsus de Liguori

FR. MARK HIGGINS

Published in 2021 by Catholic Way Publishing.
Cover & Book design by Catholic Way Publishing.

Compiled and edited by Fr. Mark Higgins. Based on the English texts "The Centenary Edition: The Complete Ascetical Works of Saint Alphonsus de Liguori, Doctor of the Church, Bishop of Saint Agatha and Founder of the Congregation of the Most Holy Redeemer" translated from the Italian by Fr. Eugene Grimm CssR.

Illustrations used in this book are works in the public domain. Front cover painting: *'Thronende Madonna und Heilige'* (Madonna and Saints Enthroned) by Alexander Maximilian Seitz, 1860. This painting depicts St. Alphonsus with St. Francis de Sales adoring Jesus Christ, Who is both in the arms of His mother and enthroned in the monstrance.

This work is published for the greater glory of Jesus Christ through His most holy mother Mary and for the sanctification of the Church militant.

Ordering Information:
Orders by trade bookstores and wholesalers.
Please contact Ingram Content at www.ingramcontent.com.

ISBN-13: 978-1-78379-523-9 (PAPERBACK)
ISBN-13: 978-1-78379-524-6 (HARDBACK)
ISBN-13: 978-1-78379-525-3 (KINDLE E-BOOK)
ISBN-13: 978-1-78379-526-0 (EPUB E-BOOK)

10 9 8 7 6 5 4 3 2 1

Available in E-Book.
www.catholicwaypublishing.com
London, England, UK
2021

"Behold the handmaid of the Lord, be it done to me according to your word."

—THE BLESSED VIRGIN MARY, THE ANNUNCIATION

Contents

The Sorrowful Mysteries

47

The Glorious Mysteries

97

The Mysteries of Light

The Hopeful Mysteries

189

Introduction

THE LIFE SPAN OF St. Alphonsus (1696-1787) covered almost the entirety of the Eighteenth Century, a century generally regarded as one of the most hostile to the Catholic Faith. On the one hand, it was the age of Jansenism; a Calvinist corruption of Catholic truth that perverted the attributes of Almighty God and rendered sanctity an unreachable and impossible goal. On the other, it was the era of 'the Enlightenment' and of so called 'enlightened monarchs', who, under the cloak of 'reason', attempted to corrupt the entire Catholic religion into a 'moral system' ordered towards decency and obedience whilst downplaying or outright denying the truths of Revelation. St. Alphonsus, through his popular devotional writings, stood on the forefront of the Catholic response to these dual blights that so threatened the salvation of souls and which continue in their influence to this day.

In response to the Jansenists, St. Alphonsus repeated without ceasing what is now referred to as 'the universal call to holiness', that fact Almighty God invites each person to co-operate with the working of His grace and to conformity with His Holy Will. An offer which, if embraced through a life of assiduous prayer, whether it is by a peasant, a king, a soldier or a merchant, will infallibly lead that individual onwards, even to the heights of sanctity. "He who prays will most certainly be saved", Alphonsus liked to repeat, "and he who does not pray, will most certainly be condemned." Alphonsus insisted, in all his ascetic works, that the cold protestant god of the Calvinistic Jansenists was completely alien to the revelation of Sacred Scripture and the interactions of those many holy mystics who conversed familiarly with Him, and whom he delights in quoting frequently.

In combatting the errors of the enlightenment rationalists, St. Alphonsus asserted the fundamental and irrefutable certainty of events of Salvation History, and moreover, of the personal destiny to either heaven or hell, and either one for eternity. The Catholic Faith was not to be seen as a merely moralistic system for good living founded by a deistic deity who cared nothing for his people. Rather, for St. Alphonsus, the core of our faith was the powerful and romantic quest by the One True God to save His people from certain damnation. A quest that consisted in the Father sending His Son, the loving saviour, to convince of us the love of God, so that, by gazing upon this love crucified, we might be converted to heartfelt contrition for our sins, and thereby avoid the certainty of Hell through a friendship with Him through the Catholic Church He founded.

In these Rosary Meditations you will experience the romanticism of St. Alphonsus as he beautifully describes the central mysteries of our Catholic Religion. The saint's 'appeal to the heart' is not however a kind of sentimentalism, provoking tears for tears' sake, but always stemming from the truths of revelation; showing the full emotive force of realities too many Catholics have allowed themselves to simply gloss over, as if they were solely historical facts only of abstract personal relevance. For the priest, the catechist, or indeed, the parent, the imagery of our saint will provide countless examples and analogies to bring to life the events of Salvation History for the benefit and edification of those being instructed. I firmly believe that no one can seriously ponder the words of St. Alphonsus without being touched and filled with the grace of compunction, being thereby brought to a deeper desire for holiness; to undertake daily mental prayer, to avoid the occasions of sin, to visit the Blessed Sacrament frequently, and to depend, more habitually, on the powerful intercession of the Immaculate Virgin.

It was by a special grace that I came across the writings of this saint when I was still an adolescent, and so he has been a saint who has accompanied me whilst at University, at Seminary and now in the Sacred Priesthood. Of all the books that I have compiled on rosary meditations, the material of this book was most familiar to me, and so, whilst Alphonsus wrote a lot on many of the mysteries of the rosary, I am very satisfied with the compilation that is presented in this volume.

Again, I have included in this work 'The Hopeful Mysteries', mysteries which I propose or offer to you for your private devotion. These mysteries cover the events of Our Lord and Our Lady prior to the Annunciation and they bring to attention many elements of Sacred Tradition so ignored and despised by rationalists and yet so dear to our Catholic forefathers. The Hopeful Mysteries are; The Creation of all things in view of Christ, the Promise of the Redeemer and the Co-Redemptrix, The Birth of Our Lady, The Presentation of Our Lady in the Temple and The Chaste Espousals of Mary and Joseph.

I would like to conclude this introduction in imitation of our holy saint, who, in a number of his works, in the midst of his narrative, makes the point that there will come a day when the writer will cease to write and the reader will cease to read. I end, therefore, these words, with the petition that you cast your mind to the soul of this poor sinner, presently writing, that you might pray for the repose of his soul. Perhaps by the time you are reading he has already passed into eternity. I hope it not presumptuous to assume the writer is in purgatory, and so, if he is still alive, pray for his perseverance and that he may die in the state of grace, fortified by the rites of the Church, and so, at least, he may arrive at that place of purification.

Yours, in the Immaculate Heart of Mary, Refuge of Sinners,
FR MARK HIGGINS

The Feast of St. Teresa of Avila, 2021
FRMARKHIGGINS@GMAIL.COM

NOTE ON PRAYING THE ROSARY USING THIS BOOK

If you are praying the rosary alone, it is suggested that you read the initial text before commencing the Our Father. Afterwards, the ten paragraphs of additional meditation can either be read before or during each Hail Mary. In a group setting a leader is required to read aloud each paragraph and commence each Hail Mary. The experience of the editor is that, in private use, with a prayerful silent reading of each passage, to say five mysteries will take at least 30 minutes and for some people closer to 45. If you feel the movements of grace pulling you into a simpler contemplation of a mystery as you read a paragraph, do not resist the Holy Spirit, and allow yourself to be at rest in the affect (the response of the heart) which Almighty God is stirring from within your soul. It is customary to commence the Holy Rosary with the Sign of the Cross, the Apostles Creed, and then, for the intentions of the Holy Father, an Our Father, a Hail Mary, and a Glory Be. After completing five mysteries we then say some concluding prayers centred around the Hail Holy Queen, these are contained at the end of each decade.

NOTE ON SOURCE MATERIAL

The texts contained in this volume were translated from the Italian by Fr. Eugene Grimm CssR. I have revised his translation myself in order to render it easier to read, understand and narrate. It still remains faithful to the Italian original. There are instances, however, where in order to ensure that the meditations for each bead have a certain completeness and succinctness, some abridgement or splicing of the saint's writings has, necessarily, been carried out. That small disclaimer having been said, the work, nonetheless, belongs entirely to our saint, all the thoughts, rhetorical devices and images are his. I hope that this abridged collection of texts drawn from St. Alphonsus' entire collection of meditation works will encourage you to obtain and read his individual works. They can be purchased in well presented and economically priced volumes through the Catholic Way Publishing website.

All images used in this book are works in the Public Domain available through Wikimedia Commons. The painting on the front cover, likewise Public Domain, depicts St. Alphonsus with St. Francis De Sales adoring Jesus Christ, Who is both in the arms of His mother and enthroned in the monstrance.

The Joyful Mysteries

The Annunciation

THE FRUIT OF THIS MYSTERY

*A holy love of God, Who became man to win
our hearts, and to save us from Hell*

EHOLD THE ARCHANGEL GABRIEL is sent as ambassador to the town of Nazareth to announce to the Virgin Mary the coming of the Word, Who desires to become incarnate in her womb. The angel salutes her, and calls her "full of grace" and "blessed among women".

The humble Virgin, chosen to be mother of the Son of God, is troubled at these praises on account of her great humility, but the angel encourages her, and tells her that she has found grace with God; that is to say, the grace which brought peace between God and man, and the reparation of the ruin caused by sin. He then tells her that she must give her son the name of Saviour, "You shall call His name Jesus" and that this, her son, is the very Son of God, Who is to redeem the world, and thus to reign over the hearts of men. Behold, at last Mary consents to be the mother of such a son, "Be it done to me according to your word." And the Eternal Word takes flesh and becomes man. Let us thank this son, and let us also thank His mother, who, in consenting to be the mother of such a son, consented also to be the mother of our salvation, and mother also of sorrows, accepting at that time the deep abyss of sorrows that it would cost her be the mother of a son who was to come to suffer and die for man.

OUR FATHER   Our Father, Who art in Heaven, hallowed be Thy name, Thy kingdom come, Thy will be done, on earth as it is in heaven. Give us this day our daily bread; and forgive us our trespasses, as we forgive those who trespass against us; and lead us not into temptation, but deliver us from evil. Amen.

HAIL MARY (10)   Hail Mary, Full of Grace, the Lord is with thee. Blessed art thou among women and blessed is the fruit of thy womb, Jesus. Holy Mary, Mother of God, pray for us sinners now, and at the hour of our death. Amen.

1. Almighty God, having determined to make Himself man in order to redeem fallen humanity, and to manifest to the world His infinite goodness, as He was about to choose on earth His mother, sought among women the holiest and the most humble. Among them all He saw one, the youthful Virgin Mary, who, as she was the most perfect in all virtues, so was she the most simple; and humble as a dove in her own esteem. "Let this one, then," said God, "be My chosen mother". God exalted her in her humility, as He Himself would later explain, "Whoever shall exalt himself shall be humbled, but the one that humbles himself shall be exalted."

2. The Lord, drawn by the odour of this humble Virgin, chose her for His mother, when He wished to become man to redeem the world. "While the King was at His repose, my spikenard sent forth its odour", thus relates the Holy Canticle. For the Blessed Virgin, like the small herb, exhaled the odour of humility; the fragrance of which ascended even to heaven, and in heaven, it, as it were, awakened Him who was in His repose, and brought Him to rest in her womb.

3. When the Archangel Gabriel announced to Mary that God had chosen her to be the mother of the Word, he said to her, "Fear not, Mary, for you have found grace with God." She did not find grace for herself, because she always possessed it, but she found it for us who had miserably lost it. Hence in order to recover grace, we should go to Mary. O Sinners, who by your sins have forfeited the divine grace, run, run to the Virgin, and say to her with confidence, "Restore to us our property which you have found."

4. The more Our Lady is exalted by the angel, the more she humbles herself, and the more she considers her nothingness. If the angel had said that she was the greatest sinner in the world, it would not have perturbed her to such a degree as this. But in hearing the exalted praises of the angel she is greatly disturbed. She was troubled because, being so full of humility, she abhorred every praise, and desired that none but her Creator, the giver of every good, should be praised and blessed. Indeed, in revelation to a saint, Mary revealed, "I disliked my own praise, and wished only to hear the praises of my God and Creator."

5. The Virgin is silent. "Take courage", says St. Bernard, addressing her, "why delay, holy Virgin, in giving your consent? The Eternal Word awaits it, in order to clothe Himself with flesh, and to become your son. We, who are all condemned to eternal death, are waiting for it in misery. If you but accept and consent to be His mother, we shall all be delivered. Quickly, oh Lady, answer; do not delay giving to the world that salvation which depends on your consent."

6. "Behold the handmaid of the Lord, be it done to me according to your word." Oh, what more beautiful, more humble, and more prudent answer could all the wisdom of men and of angels united have invented, if they had thought of it for millions of years! Oh powerful answer, which gave joy in heaven, and poured upon the earth a vast flood of graces and blessings! Answer, that hardly came forth from the humble heart of Mary before it drew from the bosom of the Eternal Father, the only begotten son, to become man in her most pure womb! Yes, for hardly had she uttered these

words when immediately the Word was made flesh: the Son of God became also the Son of Mary. Oh powerful Fiat! oh efficacious Fiat! oh Fiat to be reverenced above every Fiat! By another Fiat God created the light, the heaven, and the earth; but by this Fiat of Mary, God became man like us.

7. "And the Word was made flesh." Behold Jesus in the womb of Mary; having now made His entry into the world in all humility and obedience. He says to His Father, "Since men cannot make atonement to Your offended justice by their works and sacrifices, behold here I am, Your son, now clothed in mortal flesh, ready to satisfy for their sins with My sufferings and with My death". And so, for us miserable worms, and to captivate our love, God deigned to become man. Yes, it is a matter of faith. God has done so much in order to be loved by us.

8. Almighty God could have saved us by sending an angel to redeem us; but He wished to come Himself to die for our salvation, so that our hearts might not be divided. He wished to be both our Creator and Redeemer.

9. The prophet of old cried, "Oh that You would deign, my God to leave the heavens, and to descend here, to become man among us! Surely on beholding You like one of themselves, the mountains would melt away, the waters would burn with fire! Even the most frozen souls would be a fire with the flame of love!" But has this been the case? Have all sought to correspond with this immense love of Jesus Christ? Alas, my God, the greater part have combined to repay Him with nothing but ingratitude! And you also,

dear reader, tell me, what sort of return have you made up to now for the love your God has borne you? Have you always shown yourself thankful? Have you ever seriously reflected on the significance of it all, of God becoming man, in order to die for you?

10. Make us understand what an excess and what a miracle of love this is, that the Eternal Word, the Son of God, should have become man for the love of us. If God had created a thousand other worlds, a thousand times greater and more beautiful than the present, it is certain that this work would be infinitely less grand than the incarnation of the Word, "He has put forth His arm in strength." To execute the great work of the Incarnation, it required all the omnipotence and infinite wisdom of God; that a Divine Person should so humble Himself as to take upon Himself human nature. Thus God became man, and man became God; and hence, the divinity of the Word being united to the soul and body of Jesus Christ, all the actions of this Man-God became divine: His prayers were divine, His sufferings divine, His infant cries divine, His tears divine, His steps divine, His members divine, His very blood divine, which became, as it were, a fountain of health to wash out all our sins, and a sacrifice of infinite value to appease the justice of the Father, Who was justly offended with men.

GLORY BE TO THE FATHER   Glory be to the Father, and to the Son, and to the Holy Spirit, as it was in the beginning, is now and ever shall be, world without end. Amen.

THE FATIMA PRAYER   O my Jesus, forgive us our sins, save us from the fires of hell, lead all souls to heaven, especially those in most need of Thy mercy.

The Visitation

The visitation of Our Lady to our own souls, so that they may be sanctified

APPY IS THAT HOUSE esteemed which is visited by some royal personage, both for the honour it receives from him, and the advantages it hopes for; but more happy should be that soul which is visited by the queen of the world, most holy Mary, who cannot but fill with mercies and graces those blessed souls whom she deigns to visit with her favours. The house of Obed was blessed when it was visited by the ark of the Lord, but with how much greater blessings are those persons enriched who receive some loving visit from this living ark of God, as was the divine mother! This was experienced by the house of the Baptist, wherein scarcely had Mary entered, when she filled all that family with celestial graces and benedictions; and for this reason, the feast of the Visitation is commonly called the feast of our Lady of Graces. The divine mother is the treasurer of all graces, and so he who desires graces must have recourse to Mary.

OUR FATHER   Our Father, Who art in Heaven, hallowed be Thy name, Thy kingdom come, Thy will be done, on earth as it is in heaven. Give us this day our daily bread; and forgive us our trespasses, as we forgive those who trespass against us; and lead us not into temptation, but deliver us from evil. Amen.

HAIL MARY (10)   Hail Mary, Full of Grace, the Lord is with thee. Blessed art thou among women and blessed is the fruit of thy womb, Jesus. Holy Mary, Mother of God, pray for us sinners now, and at the hour of our death. Amen.

1. After the holy Virgin had heard from the archangel St. Gabriel, that her cousin Elizabeth had been six months pregnant, she was interiorly enlightened by the Holy Spirit to know that the Word Who had taken human flesh within her, wished to commence manifesting to the world the riches of His mercy, by imparting graces to Elizabeth's family. Therefore, without imposing any delay, rising from the quiet of her contemplation, to which she was always devoted,

and leaving her dear solitude, she immediately set out for the house of Elizabeth. Holy charity suffers all things, the grace of the Holy Spirit knows no slow movements. Not heeding the fatigue of the journey, the tender and delicate maiden quickly sets forth on her way.

2. Mary set out from Nazareth to go to the city of Hebron, seventy miles away; that is to say, at least seven days' journey over rough mountains and with no other companion than her holy spouse St. Joseph. The holy Virgin hastens, she went into the mountainous country in haste. Tell us, oh holy Lady, why did you undertake this long and difficult journey, and why did you thus hasten on you way? "I am going", she answers, "to exercise my office of charity; I am going to console a family." If, then, oh great Mother of God, your office is to console and dispense graces to souls, come to console and visit my soul. Your visit then sanctified the house of Elizabeth; come, oh Mary, and sanctify me also.

3. And behold scarcely has the Son entered into the world, when He already begins His sacrifice by beginning to suffer; but in a manner far different from that in which men suffer. Other children, while remaining in the womb of their mothers, do not suffer, because they are only in their natural place and deprived of understanding; but Jesus, while an infant, endures for nine months the darkness of that prison and endures the pain of not being able to move, and is perfectly alive to what He endures. Indeed, even from the womb, the cross on which He died was ever present to the heart of Jesus.

4. This good mother desires to aid all. Consider well this present mystery. The journey to Elizabeth was long, and in spite of how unaccustomed she was to such journeys, she immediately set forth moved by that great charity with which her most tender heart is ever filled. She went in haste, but joyful haste through her desire to help that household, hastening for the joy she felt to do good to others. And whilst she went in haste, she was in no hurry to return, rather she made her abode there for three about months.

5. He who loves God, loves all things which God loves and all men as God loves them. But as there never has been and never will be one who loves God more than Mary; so there never has been and never will be one who loves his neighbour more than Mary. The Incarnate Word, dwelling in the womb of Mary, filled His mother with charity, that she might succour all who had recourse to her. Oh, blessed among women, who excels the angels in purity, and the saints in charity! Great was the mercy of Mary towards the wretched when she was still an exile on earth; but it is far greater now that she is reigning in heaven.

6. And now the holy Virgin has arrived at the house of Elizabeth. She had been made Mother of God, but she is the first to salute her relation. Elizabeth enlightened by the Lord, already knows that the Divine Word has become man and the Son of Mary; hence she calls her blessed among women, and blesses that divine fruit that was in her womb. And, filled at the same time with confusion and joy, she exclaims, "And how is it that the mother of my Lord should come to me?" But what does the humble Mary answer to

these words? She answers, "My soul magnifies the Lord." As if she would say, "You praise me dear Elizabeth, but I praise my God that He has chosen to exalt me, His poor servant, to be His mother." Oh most holy Mary, you esteem yourself as nothing before God; but I am worse than nothing, for I am, at the same time, nothing and a sinner. You can make me humble. Make me so through love of that God Who has made you His mother.

7. Observe in this visit that Mary made to Elizabeth, the great power of the words of Mary; for at the sound of her voice the grace of the Holy Spirit was given to Elizabeth as well as to her son. Behold, how great is the power of the words of our Lady, for at the sound of them the Holy Spirit is given. Jesus is much pleased when Mary prays to Him for us. All the graces which He bestows on us through the supplications of Mary, He does not consider to be conferred on us, but rather on Mary herself. The Son is omnipotent by nature; the mother is omnipotent by grace, that is, she obtains by her prayers whatsoever she asks. This was revealed to St Bridget, who one day heard Jesus Christ addressing His mother in the following words, "Ask from Me what you wish; for your petition cannot be fruitless. Because you refused Me nothing on earth, I will refuse nothing to you in heaven."

8. The first-fruits of the redemption all passed through Mary. She was the channel by means of which grace was communicated to the Baptist, the Holy Spirit to Elizabeth, the gift of prophecy to Zechariah, and so many other blessings to that house. These were the first graces that we know

to have been given upon earth by the Word after He had become incarnate. And so we have great reason to believe that God, even from that time, had constituted Mary a universal channel, through which thenceforth should be dispensed to us all the other graces which the Lord wishes to bestow on us. Rightly then is this divine mother called the treasure, the treasurer, and the dispensatrix of divine graces. Mary is the field, in whom is found the treasure of God, that is, Jesus Christ, and with Jesus Christ the source and fountain of all graces.

9. Jesus was the fruit of Mary, as Elizabeth expressed it, "Blessed are you among women, and blessed is the fruit of your womb." Whoever, then, wishes for the fruit, must go to the tree; whoever wishes for Jesus must go to Mary; and he who finds Mary, certainly also finds Jesus. St. Elizabeth, when the most holy Virgin came to visit her in her house, not knowing how to thank her, in deep humility exclaimed, "How have I merited that the mother of my God should come to visit me?" Well did her holy cousin understand that when Mary comes she brings Jesus also; and hence it was sufficient for her to thank the mother, without naming the Son.

10. Jesus, the sweetest child, lay hidden for nine months in His mother's womb, and was awaited with eager expectation by the Virgin Mother Mary and by St. Joseph. Even whilst in the womb of Mary He saw every particular sin in review, and each sin afflicted Him immeasurably. How much did it cost Him, even from His first entrance into the world, to raise me from the ruin which I have brought on

myself by my sins. O Mother of God, help me! You had in your womb the Son of God imprisoned and confined. As, therefore, Jesus is Your prisoner, He will do everything that you tell Him. Beg Him to pardon me, ask Him to make me holy. Help me, my mother, for the sake of the favour and honour that Jesus Christ conferred upon you by dwelling within you nine months.

GLORY BE TO THE FATHER   Glory be to the Father, and to the Son, and to the Holy Spirit, as it was in the beginning, is now and ever shall be, world without end. Amen.

THE FATIMA PRAYER   O my Jesus, forgive us our sins, save us from the fires of hell, lead all souls to heaven, especially those in most need of Thy mercy.

The Nativity of Jesus Christ

THE FRUIT OF THIS MYSTERY

*Great confidence in approaching our God, sinners that
we are, seeing Him as a baby, lying in a manger*

N ORDER TO CONTEMPLATE with tenderness and
love the birth of Jesus, we must pray the Lord to
give us a lively faith. If without faith we enter
into the grotto of Bethlehem, we shall have nothing but a
feeling of compassion at seeing an infant reduced to such
a state of poverty that, being born in the depth of winter,

He is laid in a manger of beasts, without fire, and in the midst of a cold cavern. But if we enter with faith, and consider what an excess of bounty and love it was in a God to humble Himself to appear like a little child, wrapped in swadling-clothes, placed on straw, crying and shivering with cold, unable to move, depending for subsistence on His mother's milk, how is it possible that we should not feel ourselves gently constrained to give all our affections to this Infant God, Who has reduced Himself to this state to make us love Him! St. Luke says that the shepherds, after having visited Jesus in the manger, "Returned glorifying and praising God for all the things they had heard and seen." And yet what had they seen? Nothing more than a poor child trembling with cold on a little straw; but, being enlightened by faith, they recognised in this child the excess of divine love; and inflamed by this love they went on their way glorifying God, that they had the happiness to behold a God Who had emptied Himself and annihilated Himself for the love of men.

OUR FATHER   Our Father, Who art in Heaven, hallowed be Thy name, Thy kingdom come, Thy will be done, on earth as it is in heaven. Give us this day our daily bread; and forgive us our trespasses, as we forgive those who trespass against us; and lead us not into temptation, but deliver us from evil. Amen.

HAIL MARY (10)   Hail Mary, Full of Grace, the Lord is with thee. Blessed art thou among women and blessed is the fruit of thy womb, Jesus. Holy Mary, Mother of

God, pray for us sinners now, and at the hour of our death. Amen.

1. "Man does not love Me", God would seem to say, "because he does not see Me. I wish to make Myself seen by him and to converse with him, and so make Myself loved." The divine love for man was extreme, and so it had been from all eternity. All the creatures God had made were so many darts of love to the heart of man; but God was not satisfied with these darts only; they were not enough to gain Him the love of men. "He has made Me as a chosen arrow; in His quiver He has hidden Me." Just as the sportsman keeps in reserve the best arrow for the last shot, in order to secure his prey; so did God among all His gifts keep Jesus in reserve till the fullness of time should come, and then He sent Him as a last dart to wound with love the hearts of men. Jesus, then, was the choice and reserved arrow, powerful enough to bring nations to their knees. Oh may I be among that number of stricken hearts, burning with love before the manger of Bethlehem and before the Holy Presence of the Blessed Sacrament on our altars.

2. God had decreed that His son should be born, not in the house of Joseph, but in a cave and stable for animals, in the poorest and most painful way that a child can be born; and therefore He so disposed events that Caesar should publish an edict that every one should go and enrol himself in the city whence he drew his origin. When Joseph heard this order he was much agitated as to whether he should leave or take with him the Virgin Mother, as she was now near childbirth. "My spouse and my lady", St. Joseph said to her,

"on the one hand I should not wish to leave you alone; on the other, if I take you, I am afflicted at the thought that you will have to suffer much during this long journey, and in such severe weather. My poverty will not permit me to conduct you with that comfort which you require." But Mary answers him, and encourages him with these words, "My Joseph, do not fear; I shall go with you; the Lord will assist us." She knew, by divine inspiration, and also because she was well versed in the prophecy of Micah, that the Divine Infant was to be born in Bethlehem. She therefore takes the swathing bands, and the other poor garments already prepared, and departs with Joseph.

3. My dear Redeemer, I know that in this journey You were accompanied by hosts of angels from Heaven; but here on earth, who was there to bear You company? You have only Joseph, and Mary, who carries You within herself. Disdain not, O my Jesus, to let me also accompany You, miserable and ungrateful as I have been. I now see the wrong I have done You; You came down from Heaven to make Yourself my companion on earth, and I, by my frequent offences, have ungratefully left You! I repent with all my soul of having so often turned my back upon You and forsaken You. I purpose and I hope, through Your grace, never more to leave You, or separate myself from You again.

4. Let us now consider all the devout and holy discourses which these two holy spouses must have held together during this journey to Bethlehem concerning the mercy, goodness, and love of the Divine Word, who was shortly to be born, and to appear on the earth for the salvation of

men. Let us also consider the praises, the benedictions, the thanksgivings, the acts of humility and love, which these two illustrious pilgrims uttered on the way. This holy Virgin, so soon to become a mother, certainly suffered much in so long a journey, made in the middle of winter, and over rough roads; but she suffered with peace and with love. She offered to God all these her trials, uniting them to those of Jesus, whom she carried in her womb. Oh, let us also unite ourselves with Mary and Joseph, and accompany them in the journey of our life; and, with them, let us accompany the King of Heaven, Who is about to be born in a cave, and make His first appearance in the world as an Infant, but an Infant the poorest and most forsaken that was ever born amongst men. And let us beseech Jesus, Mary, and Joseph, that, through the merits of the sufferings which they endured in this journey, they would accompany us in the journey that we are making to eternity. Oh, happy shall we be, if in life and in death, we are always accompanied by these three great personages!

5. For this end was it decreed by God that the edict of Caesar should come forth; namely, that His son should not only be born poor, but the poorest of men, causing Him to be born away from His own house, in a cave which was inhabited only by animals. Other poor people, who are born in their own house, have certainly more comforts in the way of clothes, of fire, and the assistance of persons who lend their aid, even if it is out of compassion. What son of a poor person was ever born in a stable? In a stable only beasts are born. St. Luke relates how it happened. The time being come that Mary was to be delivered, Joseph goes

to seek some lodging for her in Bethlehem. He goes about and inquires at every house, and he finds none. He tries to find one in an inn, but neither does he find any there. Mary was obliged to take shelter and bring forth her son in a cave where, notwithstanding the gathering of people in that city, there was nobody else present; there were only two animals. When the sons of princes are born, they have warm rooms prepared for them, adorned with hangings, silver cradles, the finest clothes, and they are waited on by the highest nobles and ladies of the kingdom. The King of heaven, instead of a warm and beautiful room, has nothing but a cold grotto, whose only ornament is the grass that grows there; instead of a bed of feathers, He has nothing but a little hard sharp straw; instead of fine garments, He has but a few poor rough cold and damp rags. Instead of a fire, and of the attendance of great people, He has but the warm breath and the company of two animals; finally, in place of the silver cradle, He must lie in a vile manger. He who encompasses all things in His embrace is laid in the manger of brute cattle. Yes, for this King of kings wished to be poor, and the poorest of all. Even the children of the poor have milk enough provided for them, but Jesus Christ wished to be poor ever in this; for God, in order to comply with the desire of His son, Who wished to be poor in everything, did not provide Mary with milk in abundance, but only with as much as would barely suffice to sustain the life of His son; whence the holy Church sings in her liturgy, "He was fed on a little milk."

6. No sooner had Mary entered the cavern than she began to pray; and the hour of her delivery being come, behold

she sees a great light, and feels in her heart a heavenly joy. She casts down her eyes, and, what does she see? An Infant so tender and beautiful that He fills her with love! But He trembles and cries and stretches out His arms to show that He desires that she should take Him up into her bosom. "I stretched forth My hands to seek the caresses of My Mother", Jesus said to St. Bridget. Mary then calls Joseph, "Come Joseph, come and see, for the Son of God is now born." The holy old man enters, and prostrating himself, weeps for joy. Mary, holding Him to her bosom, adores Him as her God, kissing His face as her Child.

7. What tidings could be a greater joy to a race of poor exiles condemned to death, than to be told that their Saviour was come, not only to deliver them from death, but to obtain for them liberty to return to their own country? And this is what the angels announce, that Jesus Christ is born for us, to deliver us from everlasting death, and to open Heaven for us, our true country, from which we were banished because of our sins. Let us arise with those shepherds and enter, the door is open. The Cave is open and without guards or doors, so that all may go in when they please to seek Him and to speak to Him, and even to embrace their Infant King if they love and desire Him. Lord, I should not have dared to approach You seeing myself so deformed by sin; but since You, my Jesus, invite me so courteously, and call me so lovingly, I will not refuse. After having so many times turned my back upon You I will not add a fresh insult by refusing, out of distrust, this affectionate, this loving invitation.

8. Let every soul, then, enter the Cave of Bethlehem. Behold and see that tender Infant, Who is weeping as He lies in the manger on that miserable straw. See how beautiful He is, look at the light which He sends forth, and the love which He breathes; those eyes send out arrows which wound the hearts that desire Him, the very stable, the very straw cry out and tell you to love Him Who loves you, to love God Who is infinite Love, and Who came down from Heaven, and Made Himself a little Child, and became poor, to make you understand the love He bears you, and to gain your love by His sufferings. The shepherds who came to visit Him in the stable of Bethlehem brought their gifts; you must also bring your gifts. What will you bring Him? The most acceptable present you can bring Him is that of a contrite and loving heart.

9. Christ chose to be laid in the manger where the animals were fed, to make us understand that He had become man also to make Himself our Food. In the manger, where the food of animals is placed, He allowed His limbs to be laid, thereby showing that His own body would be the eternal food of men. Besides this, He is born every day in the Blessed Sacrament in the hands of the priest at holy Mass; the Altar is the Crib, and there we go to feed ourselves on His flesh. Faith teaches us that, when we receive Communion, the same Jesus Who was in the manger of Bethlehem is not merely in our arms, but in our breasts. He was born for this purpose, to give Himself entirely to us, "A child is born to us, a son is given to us."

10. Jesus chose at His birth the stable of Bethlehem for His hermitage and oratory; and for this purpose He so disposed events as to be born out of the city in a solitary cave, in order to recommend to us the love of solitude and of silence. Jesus remains in silence in the manger; Mary and Joseph adore and contemplate Him in silence. It was revealed to a great saint that all that passed in the cave of Bethlehem, even the visit of the shepherds and the adoration of the holy Magi, took place in silence, and without a word. The Infant Jesus does not speak; but oh! How much His silence says! Oh, blessed is He that converses with Jesus, Mary, and Joseph, in this holy solitude of the manger. The shepherds, through admitted there but for a very short time, came out from the stable all inflamed with love to God; for they did nothing but praise and bless Him. Oh, happy the soul that shuts itself up in the solitude of Bethlehem to contemplate the divine mercy, and the love that God has borne, and still bears, to men! "I will lead her into the wilderness, and I will speak to her heart." There the divine Infant will speak, not to the ear, but to the heart, inviting the soul to love a God Who has loved her so much. When we see there the poverty of this wandering little hermit, Who remains in that cold cave, without fire, with a manger for a crib, and a little straw for a bed; when we hear the cries, and behold the tears of this innocent Child, and consider that He is our God, how is it possible to think of anything but of loving Him! Oh, what a sweet hermitage for a soul that has faith in the stable of Bethlehem! Let us also imitate Mary and Joseph, who, burning with love, remain contemplating the great Son of God clothed in flesh, let us meditate on the divine majesty shrouded beneath the form of a little

Infant, despised and forsaken by the world, and Who does and suffers everything in order to make Himself loved by men, and let us beseech Him to admit us into this sacred retreat; there stop, there remain, and never leave it again.

GLORY BE TO THE FATHER   Glory be to the Father, and to the Son, and to the Holy Spirit, as it was in the beginning, is now and ever shall be, world without end. Amen.

THE FATIMA PRAYER   O my Jesus, forgive us our sins, save us from the fires of hell, lead all souls to heaven, especially those in most need of Thy mercy.

The Purification of Mary and the Presentation of the Infant Christ in the Temple

---

THE FRUIT OF THIS MYSTERY

To embrace the humiliations of being thought and known as a sinner

 LTHOUGH MARY WAS NOT bound by the law of Purification, since she was always a virgin and always pure, yet her humility and obedience made

29

her wish to go like other mothers to purify herself. She at the same time obeyed the second precept, to present and offer her son to the Eternal Father. But the Blessed Virgin did not offer Him as other mothers offered their sons. Others, indeed, offered them to God; but they knew that this oblation was simply a legal ceremony, and that by redeeming them they made them their own, without fear of having again to offer them to death. Mary really offered her son to death, and knew for certain that the sacrifice of the life of Jesus which she then made was one day to be actually consummated on the Altar of the Cross; so that Mary, by offering the life of her son, came, in consequence of the love she bore this son, really to sacrifice her own entire self to God.

OUR FATHER   Our Father, Who art in Heaven, hallowed be Thy name, Thy kingdom come, Thy will be done, on earth as it is in heaven. Give us this day our daily bread; and forgive us our trespasses, as we forgive those who trespass against us; and lead us not into temptation, but deliver us from evil. Amen.

HAIL MARY (10)   Hail Mary, Full of Grace, the Lord is with thee. Blessed art thou among women and blessed is the fruit of thy womb, Jesus. Holy Mary, Mother of God, pray for us sinners now, and at the hour of our death. Amen.

1. The time having now come when, according to the law, Mary had to go to the Temple for her purification, and to present Jesus to the Divine Father, behold she sets out in company with Joseph. Joseph carries the two turtle-doves

that they are to offer to God, and Mary carries her dear Infant: she takes the Lamb of God to offer Him to the Almighty, in token of the great sacrifice that this son should one day accomplish on the cross.

2. Consider the holy Virgin entering the Temple; she makes an oblation of her son on the part of the whole human race. The offering of Mary is joined to that of Jesus. "Behold me" (says also the holy Infant), "behold Me, O My Father; to You do I consecrate My whole life; You have sent Me into the world to save it by My blood; behold My blood, My whole self. I offer Myself entirely to You for the salvation of the world." No sacrifice was ever so acceptable to God as this which His dear son then made to Him; Who had become, even from His infancy, a victim and priest. If all men and angels had offered their lives, their oblation could not have been so dear to God as was this of Jesus Christ, because in this offering alone the Eternal Father received infinite honour and infinite satisfaction.

3. Already the most Blessed Virgin was enlightened by the Sacred Scriptures, and knew the sufferings that the Redeemer was to endure in His life, and still more at the time of His death. But in the words of Simeon, "And a sword shall pierce your own soul" all the minute circumstances of the sufferings, internal and external, that were to torment her Jesus in His Passion, were made known to her. She consented to all with a constancy which filled even the angels with astonishment; she re-pronounced the sentence that her son should die, and die by so ignominious and painful a death, saying, "Eternal Father, since You will that it should

be so, 'Not my will, but Yours be done.' I unite my will to Your most holy will, and I sacrifice this, my son to You. I am satisfied that He should lose His life for Your glory and the salvation of the world. At the same time I sacrifice my heart to You, that it may be transpierced with sorrow, and this as much as it pleases You. It suffices me, my God, that You are glorified and satisfied with my offering." "Not my will, but Yours be done!" O charity without measure! O constancy without parallel! O victory which deserves the eternal admiration of Heaven and earth!

4. Forty days after the birth of our Lord, that she might fulfil the precepts of legal purification, the Blessed Virgin offered her divine son in the Temple, and placed Him in the arms of the aged Simeon. Mary had no need to be purified, because she was always free from every stain; but in order to obey the law, and through humility, she went to be purified, and to appear sullied like other women. Since, then, the Mother of God, who was so pure, was not ashamed to appear as if she needed to be purified, how shall we ever be ashamed to confess our sins or be thought of as sinners. Help us O Blessed Mother to overcome all these prideful imperfections.

5. As Almighty God willed that His Divine Word should only become man by the express consent of Mary, so also He willed the sacrifice of His life for our salvation should only occur with the assent of Mary; that, together with the sacrifice of the life of the Son, the mother's heart might also be sacrificed. The quality of mother gives her a special right over her children; hence, Jesus being in Himself innocent and undeserving of punishment, it seemed fitting that He

should not be condemned to the Cross as a Victim for the sins of the world without the consent of His mother, by which she should willingly offer Him to death. But although from the moment she became the mother of Jesus, Mary consented to His death, yet God willed that on this day she should make a solemn sacrifice of herself by offering her son to Him in the Temple, sacrificing His precious life to Divine Justice.

6. Behold Mary on the road to Jerusalem to offer her son; she hastens her steps towards the place of sacrifice and she herself bears the beloved Victim in her arms. She enters the Temple, approaches the altar, and there, beaming with modesty, devotion, and humility, presents her son to the Most High. In the meantime the holy Simeon who had received a promise from God that he should not die without having first seen the expected Messiah, takes the Divine Child from the arms of the Blessed Virgin, and, enlightened by the Holy Spirit, announces to her how much the sacrifice she then made of her son would cost her, and that with Him her own blessed soul would also be sacrificed.

7. Ah, most sorrowful mother, had you loved your son less, or had He been less amiable, or had He loved you less, your sufferings in offering Him to death would certainly have been diminished. But there never was, and never will be, a mother who loved her son more than you loved yours; for there never was, and never will be a son more amiable, or one who loved his mother more than your Jesus loved you. O God, had we beheld the beauty, the majesty of the countenance of that Divine Child, could we have ever had

the courage to sacrifice His life for our own salvation? But Mary not only offered her son to death in the Temple, but she renewed that offering every moment of her life; for she revealed to St. Bridget that the sorrow announced to her by the holy Simeon never left her heart until her Assumption into Heaven.

8. Holy Simeon received a promise from God that he should not die until he had seen the Messiah born. But this grace he only received through Mary, for it was in her arms that he found the Saviour. Hence, he who desires to find Jesus, will not find Him otherwise than by Mary. Let us, then, go to this Divine Mother if we wish to find Jesus, and let us go with great confidence.

9. As the stag, wounded by an arrow, carries the pain with him wherever he goes, because he carries with him the arrow that has wounded him; thus the divine mother, after the prophecy of holy Simeon, always carried her sorrow with her by the continual remembrance of the passion of her son. Your mind, oh Mary, and your thoughts, tinged in the blood of the passion of our Lord, were always moved with sorrow as if they actually saw the blood flowing from His wounds. Thus her son Himself was that arrow in the heart of Mary, Who, the more worthy of love He showed Himself to her, always wounded her the more with the sorrowful thought that she should lose Him by so cruel a death.

10. Herod having heard that the expected Messiah was born, foolishly feared that the new-born King would deprive him of his kingdom. An angel appeared in a dream to St.

Joseph, and said to him, "Arise, and take the child and His mother, and fly into Egypt." Immediately, on that very night, Joseph made this command known to Mary; and taking the infant Jesus, they commenced their journey. Must He, then, Who came to save men flee from men? And then the afflicted Mary knew that already the prophecy of Simeon, regarding her son, was beginning to be verified, "He is set for a sign which shall be contradicted." What suffering it must have been to the heart of Mary, to hear the tidings of that cruel exile of herself with her son! "Flee from Your friends to strangers, from the holy temple of the only true God, to the temples of demons." What greater tribulation than that a new-born child, clinging to its mother's bosom, should be forced to fly with the mother herself! The sight of Jesus and Mary wandering like fugitives through this world, teaches us that we should live as pilgrims on earth, detached from the goods which the world offers us, as having soon to leave them and go to eternity. It also teaches us to embrace crosses, for we cannot live in this world without a cross.

GLORY BE TO THE FATHER   Glory be to the Father, and to the Son, and to the Holy Spirit, as it was in the beginning, is now and ever shall be, world without end. Amen.

THE FATIMA PRAYER   O my Jesus, forgive us our sins, save us from the fires of hell, lead all souls to heaven, especially those in most need of Thy mercy.

The Finding of the Boy Jesus in the Temple

THE FRUIT OF THIS MYSTERY

Perfect contrition for ours sins, which separate us from Christ

T HE BLESSED VIRGIN AND St. Joseph, having gone to Jerusalem to visit the Temple, took with them the child Jesus; but at the return they lost Him. For three days, then, they sought after Him with many sighs and tears, and found Him at last in the Temple. The Blessed

Virgin never lost the grace of her Divine Son; she was only deprived of His sensible presence; and, nevertheless, she sought after Him with tears. Oh, how much greater reason has the sinner to search with tears for Jesus Christ, when he has lost His grace! Whoever seeks for Him in this way will surely find Him.

OUR FATHER   Our Father, Who art in Heaven, hallowed be Thy name, Thy kingdom come, Thy will be done, on earth as it is in heaven. Give us this day our daily bread; and forgive us our trespasses, as we forgive those who trespass against us; and lead us not into temptation, but deliver us from evil. Amen.

HAIL MARY (10)   Hail Mary, Full of Grace, the Lord is with thee. Blessed art thou among women and blessed is the fruit of thy womb, Jesus. Holy Mary, Mother of God, pray for us sinners now, and at the hour of our death. Amen.

1. Our blessed Redeemer passed His first infancy in Egypt, leading there, for seven years, a life of poverty and contempt. Joseph and Mary were both strangers and unknown there, having there neither relatives nor friends; and they could hardly earn their daily bread by the labour of their hands. Their cottage was poor, their bed was poor, and their food was poor. In this hut Mary weaned Jesus. First she fed Him from her breast; and afterwards with her hands she took from the bowl a little bread soaked in water, and then she put it in the sacred mouth of her son. In this cottage she made Him His first little garment; she took off His swaddling-clothes and began to dress Him. In this cottage the

Child Jesus began to take His first steps; but He kept falling many times and trembling, as it happens to other children. Here He began to utter His first words, but in stammering. O wonder! To what has not God reduced Himself for the love of us! A God trembling and falling as He walks! a God stammering whilst He speaks! Not unlike this was the poor and abject life Jesus led on His return from Egypt to the house of Nazareth. Until the age of thirty He held no other office than that of a simple shop-boy, being obedient to Joseph and Mary.

2. The Blessed Virgin was accustomed to visit the temple every year at the paschal season, with Joseph her spouse and Jesus. Once, when Jesus was about twelve years old, He remained in Jerusalem, though she was not aware of it, for she thought He was in company with others. When she reached Nazareth she inquired for her son, and not finding Him there, she returned immediately to Jerusalem to seek Him, but did not succeed until after three days. Now let us imagine what distress that afflicted mother must have experienced in those three days in which she was searching everywhere for her son, but heard no news of Him. Oh, with how much greater tenderness must Mary, overcome with fatigue, and yet not having found her beloved son, have repeated those words of Ruben, concerning his brother Joseph, "The boy does not appear, and where shall I go to?", "My Jesus does not appear, and I know not what to do that I may find Him; but where shall I go without my treasure?" Weeping continually, she repeated during these three days with David, "My tears have been my bread day and night, whilst it is said to me daily, 'where is Your God?'"

During those nights the afflicted mother had no rest, but wept and prayed without ceasing to God, that He would enable her to find her son.

3. Often during that time Our Lady repeated to her son in prayer the words of the spouse in the Canticle, "Show me where You feed, where You lie in the midday, lest I begin to wander." That is, "My son, tell me where You are, that I may no longer wander, seeking You in vain." And again, with tears, she then exclaimed, "Ah, the light of my eyes, my dear Jesus, is no more with me; He is far from me, I know not where He is!" Through the love which this holy mother bore her son, she suffered more at this loss of Jesus than any martyr ever suffered at death. Ah, how long were these three days for Mary! They appeared three ages. They were very bitter days, for there was none to comfort her. "And who", she exclaimed with Jeremiah, "who can console me if He who could console me is far from me? And therefore my eyes are not satisfied with weeping."

4. He who is born blind is little sensible of the pain of being deprived of the light of day; but to him who has once had sight and enjoyed the light, it is a great sorrow to find himself deprived of it by blindness. And thus it is with those unhappy souls who, being blinded by the mire of this earth, have but little knowledge of God, and therefore scarcely feel pain at not finding Him. On the contrary, the man who, illuminated with celestial light, has been made worthy to find by love the sweet presence of the highest good, oh God, how he mourns when he finds himself deprived of it! And so, how great was the pain of Our Lady and Saint Joseph when

Jesus was lost in the temple! They were accustomed to the enjoyment of the sweet presence of their beloved Saviour. What, then, must have been their sorrow when they were deprived of it for three days, without knowing whether they should evermore find Jesus, and most painful of all, without knowing why they had lost Him. How great, on the other hand, was their joy when they found Jesus and realised that the absence of the Child did not arise from any neglect on their part, but from a zeal for the glory of the Father.

5. The sorrowful mother was grieved to find Jesus withdrawn from her, for her humility made her consider herself unworthy to remain with Him any longer, and attend upon Him on earth, and have the care of such a treasure. And perhaps, she may have thought within herself, I have not served Him as I ought. Perhaps I have been guilty of some neglect, and therefore He has left me. They sought Him, lest He perchance had left them. Certainly there is no greater grief for a soul that loves God than the fear of having displeased Him. And therefore Mary never complained in any other sorrow but this, lovingly expostulating with Jesus after she found Him, "Son, why have You done so to us? Your father and I have sought You sorrowing." By these words she wished to make known to Him the grief she had experienced during His absence from her, on account of the love she bore Him.

6. Most holy Mary lost her son for three days: during that time she wept continually for having lost sight of Jesus, and did not cease to seek after Him till she found Him. How then does it happen that so many sinners not only lose sight of Jesus, but even lose His divine grace; and instead

of weeping for so great a loss, sleep in peace, and make no effort to recover so great a blessing? They who do so clearly do not understand the malice of mortal sin and the value of grace. Divine grace is an infinite treasure, because it makes us friends of God. Hence it follows, that if there cannot be a greater happiness than to enjoy the grace of God, there cannot be a greater misery than to incur His displeasure by sin, which makes us His enemies. Mary obtains for sinners, by her intercession, the gift of grace; she restores them to life. All you who desire the kingdom of God; honour the Virgin Mary, and you shall have life and eternal salvation. If we have been so unfortunate as to lose divine grace, strive to recover it, but to strive through Mary; for if we have lost it, she has found it.

7. "And He went down to Nazareth and was subject to them." Jesus went to fetch the water; Jesus opened and shut up the shop; Jesus swept the house; He collected the fragments of wood for the fire, and worked all day, helping Joseph in His labours. O wonder! A God serving as a boy! A God sweeping the house! A God working and sweating to plane a piece of wood! And Who is this? The omnipotent God, Who by a nod created the world, and can destroy it when He pleases! Ought not the mere thought of this to move our hearts to love Him? How sweet it must have been to observe the devotion with which Jesus said prayers, the patience with which He laboured, the promptitude with which He obeyed, the modesty with which He took His food, and the sweetness and affability with which He spoke and conversed! Oh, every word, every action of Jesus was so

holy that it filled every one with love for Him; but especially Mary and Joseph, who were constantly observing Him!

8. Look at Jesus growing towards manhood, how busily He toils and labours, in helping Joseph in his trade of a carpenter! Who can ever attentively consider Jesus, that beautiful youth, fatiguing and exhausting Himself in bringing into form some rough-hewn piece of wood, and not exclaim, "But, most sweet youth, are You not that God, Who by a word did create the world out of nothing? And how comes it that You have laboured now for a whole day, bathed in sweat, to fashion this piece of wood, and even still Your work remains unfinished? What has reduced You to such a state of weakness? O Holy Faith! O Divine Love! O God! O God!" How such a thought as this, if once well mastered, would suffice, not only to inflame us, but to reduce us, so to speak, to ashes with the fire of love!

9. The Lord advanced also in grace with men, increasing in beauty and amiability. Oh, how Jesus showed Himself more and more amiable every day of His youth, showing more and more every day the claims He had upon men's love! With what delight did the holy youth obey Mary and Joseph! With what recollection of mind did He work! With what moderation did He partake of food! With what modesty did He speak! With what sweetness and affability did He converse with all! With what devotion did He pray! In a word, every action, every word, every movement of Jesus, inflamed with love the hearts of all those who beheld Him, and especially of Mary and Joseph, who had the good fortune to see Him always at their side. Oh, how

these holy spouses remained always intent in contemplating and admiring the operations, the words, and gestures of this Man-God!

10. Consider what a flame of holy love must have been kindled in the heart of Joseph by meditating on all these things, and in seeing his Lord performing for him all the little offices of a boy. What affection must he have felt in carrying Jesus in his arms, caressing Him, and in receiving the caresses of that sweet Infant! In hearing from Him the words of Eternal Life, which, like so many loving darts, wounded his heart! And particularly in witnessing the holy examples of all virtues which the divine Child gave him. Long familiarity with persons who love one another cools their affection; for the longer men converse together, the more perfectly they learn one another's defects. This was not the case with Joseph; the more he conversed with Jesus, the better he became acquainted with His sanctity. Consider, then, how great was Joseph's love for Jesus, since, according to the authors, he enjoyed His company for the space of twenty-five years. My holy St. Joseph, pray to Jesus for me. Having obeyed all Your commands on earth, He will certainly never refuse anything You ask of Him. Tell Him to pardon me the offences that I have offered to Him. Tell Him to detach me from creatures and from myself; ask Him to inflame me with His holy love; and then let Him treat me as He pleases. And you, O most holy Mary, through the love which Joseph bore you, take me under your patronage, and beg of this your spouse to accept me for his servant.

GLORY BE TO THE FATHER   Glory be to the Father, and to the Son, and to the Holy Spirit, as it was in the beginning, is now and ever shall be, world without end. Amen.

THE FATIMA PRAYER   O my Jesus, forgive us our sins, save us from the fires of hell, lead all souls to heaven, especially those in most need of Thy mercy.

CONCLUDING PRAYERS   *Upon completing the recitation of the Holy Rosary, the following prayers are customary, but others too may be added according to one's devotion and preference.*

HAIL HOLY QUEEN   Hail Holy Queen, Mother of Mercy, hail our life, our sweetness and our hope. To thee do we cry, poor banished children of Eve, to thee do we send up our sighs, mourning and weeping in this vale of tears. Turn then, most gracious advocate, thine eyes of mercy towards us, and after this, our exile, show unto us the blessed fruit of thy womb, Jesus. O clement, O loving, O sweet Virgin Mary. Pray for us O holy Mother of God, that we may be made worthy of the promises of Christ.

Let Us Pray   O God, Whose only begotten son, by His life, death and resurrection, has purchased for us the rewards of eternal life, grant we beseech You, that meditating on these mysteries of the most Holy Rosary of the Blessed Virgin Mary, we may both imitate what they contain and obtain what they promise, through the same Christ our Lord. Amen.

PRAYER TO SAINT MICHAEL THE ARCHANGEL   Holy
Michael, the Archangel, defend us in the day of battle. Be
our safeguard against the wickedness and snares of the devil.
May God rebuke him, we humbly pray; and do thou, O
Prince of the heavenly hosts, by the power of God thrust
down into hell Satan and all the evil spirits who wander
through the world seeking the ruin of souls. Amen.

MEMORARE   Remember, O most gracious Virgin Mary,
that never was it known that anyone who fled to thy protection, implored thy help, or sought thine intercession was
left unaided. Inspired by this confidence, I fly unto thee,
O Virgin of virgins, my mother; to thee do I come, before
you I stand, sinful and sorrowful. O Mother of the Word
Incarnate, despise not my petitions, but in thy mercy hear
and answer me. Amen.

May the Divine Assistance remain always with us, and may
the souls of the faithful departed, through the mercy of God
rest in peace. Amen.

The Sorrowful Mysteries

The Agony in the Garden

THE FRUIT OF THIS MYSTERY

Sorrow at the sight of the sins of humanity, including one's own

EHOLD, OUR MOST LOVING Saviour, having come to the Garden of Gethsemane, did of His own accord make a beginning of His bitter Passion by giving full liberty to the passions of fear, of weariness, and of sorrow to come and afflict Him with all their torments, "He began to fear; and to be heavy, to grow sorrowful, and to be sad." He began, then, first to feel a great fear of death, and of the sufferings He would have soon to endure. "He began to fear", but how? Was it not He Himself that had offered Himself spontaneously to endure all these torments? "He was offered because He willed it." Was it not He who had so much desired this hour of His Passion, and who had said shortly before, "With desire have I desired to eat this Pasch with you?" And yet how is it that He was seized with such a fear of death, that He even prayed His Father to deliver Him from it? He prays that the chalice may pass from Him, in order to show that He was truly man. He, our loving Saviour, chose indeed to die for us in order by His death to prove to us the love that He bore us; but in order that men might not suppose that He had assumed a fantastic body, or that by virtue of His divinity He had died without suffering any pain, He therefore made this prayer to His Heavenly Father, not indeed with a view of being heard, but to give us to understand that He died as man, and afflicted with a great fear of death and of the sufferings which should accompany His death. O most amiable Jesus! You would have, then, taken upon Yourself our fearfulness in order to give us Your courage in suffering the trials of this life. May You be forever blessed for Your great mercy and love! May all our hearts love You as much as You desire, and as much as You deserve!

OUR FATHER   Our Father, Who art in Heaven, hallowed be Thy name, Thy kingdom come, Thy will be done, on earth as it is in heaven. Give us this day our daily bread; and forgive us our trespasses, as we forgive those who trespass against us; and lead us not into temptation, but deliver us from evil. Amen.

HAIL MARY (10)   Hail Mary, Full of Grace, the Lord is with thee. Blessed art thou among women and blessed is the fruit of thy womb, Jesus. Holy Mary, Mother of God, pray for us sinners now, and at the hour of our death. Amen.

1. The Blessed Virgin revealed to St. Bridget that at the time when the Passion of our Lord was drawing nigh, her eyes were always filled with tears, as she thought of her beloved son Whom she was about to lose on this earth. A cold sweat covered her body from the fear that seized her at the prospect of His approaching suffering. Behold, the appointed day at length arrived, and Jesus comes in tears to take leave of His mother before He begins His passion. St. Bonaventure, contemplating Mary on that night, says, "You spent it without sleep, and while others slept, You remained watching."

2. Knowing that the hour of His Passion had now come, after having washed the feet of His disciples and instituted the most Holy Sacrament of the Altar, wherein He left us His whole self, Our Lord Jesus goes to the Garden of Gethsemane, to where He knew that His enemies would come to arrest Him. He there betakes Himself to prayer, and lo! He finds Himself assailed by a great dread, by a great repugnance, and by a great sadness. Frequently go, O devout reader, to the garden of Gethsemane, after the example of St. Teresa of Avila, who used to say that she always found Him there alone. Consider Jesus in His affliction, as He falls into an agony, sweats blood, and declares His sorrow to be such as to be enough to cause Him to die. There, in the garden you will readily find comfort in any afflictions of

your own, seeing that He endures it all out of His love for you. And at that sight of Jesus preparing Himself to die for you, do you likewise prepare yourself to die for Him; and when you experience in your distresses more affliction than usual, then say the words St. Thomas the Apostle said to the other disciples, "Let us also go, that we may die with Him."

3. As soon as they had said grace, Jesus leaves the supper room with His disciples, goes into the garden of Gethsemane, and begins to pray. But, alas, at the commencement of His prayer, He is assailed with a great fear, an oppressive heaviness, and an overwhelming sadness. Hence our Redeemer, overwhelmed with sadness, said that His blessed soul was sorrowful even unto death. Then was presented before Him the melancholy scene of all the torments and ignominies which were prepared for Him. In His Passion these afflicted Him one by one; but in the garden, the punches, the spittle, the scourges, the thorns, the nails, and the reproaches which He was to suffer, came all together to torment Him. He there embraced them all, but in embracing them, He trembled, He agonised, and He prayed. But, my Jesus, who compels You to submit to such torments? "The love", He answers, "which I bear to men constrains Me to endure them." Ah, how great must have been the astonishment of heaven at the sight of omnipotence become weak, of the joy of paradise oppressed with sadness! A God afflicted! And why? To save men, His own creatures.

4. We read in history that several penitents being enlightened by divine light to see the malice of their sins, have died of pure sorrow for them. Oh, what torment, then, must not the

heart of Jesus endure at the sight of all the sins of the world, of all the blasphemies, sacrileges, acts of impurity, and all the other crimes which should be committed by men after His death, every one of which, like a wild beast, tore His heart separately by its own malice. For that reason, our afflicted Lord, during His agony in the garden, exclaimed, "Is this, therefore, O men, the reward that you render Me for My immeasurable love? Oh, if I could only see that, grateful for My affection, you gave up sin and began to love Me, with what delight should I not have to die for you! But to behold, after all My sufferings, so many sins; after so much love, such ingratitude; this is what afflicts Me the most, makes Me sorrowful even unto death, and makes Me sweat pure blood." Indeed, this bloody sweat was so copious that it first bathed all the vestments of our Blessed Redeemer, and then came forth in quantity and bathed the ground.

5. Ah, my loving Jesus, I do not behold in this garden either scourges or thorns or nails that pierce You; how, then, is it that I see You all bathed in blood from Your head to Your feet? Alas, my sins were the cruel press which, by dint of affliction and sorrow, drew so much blood from Your heart. I was, then, one of Your most cruel executioners, who contributed the most to crucify You with my sins. It is certain that, if I had sinned less, You, my Jesus, would have have suffered less. As much pleasure, therefore, as I have taken in offending You, so much the more did I increase the sorrow of Your heart, already full of anguish. How, then, does not this thought make me die of grief, when I see that I have repaid the love You have shown me in Your Passion by adding to Your sorrow and suffering? I, then, have tormented this

heart, so loving and so worthy of love, which has shown so much love to me. My Lord, since I have now no other means left of consoling You than to weep over my offences towards You, I will now, my Jesus, sorrow for them and lament over them with my whole heart. Oh, give me, I pray You, so great sorrow for them as may make me to my last breath weep over the displeasure I have caused You, my God, my Love my All.

6. Jesus, beholding Himself charged with the burden of satisfying for all the sins of the world, prostrated Himself, with His face on the ground, to pray for men, as if He were ashamed to raise His eyes towards heaven, loaded as He was with such iniquities. O my Redeemer, I behold You pale and worn out with sorrow; You are in the agony of death, and You pray. Tell me, my Saviour, for whom do You pray? Ah, You did not pray so much for Yourself at that hour as for me! You offered to Your Eternal Father Your all-powerful prayers, united to Your sufferings, to obtain for me, a wretched sinner, the pardon of my sins. Now, O my Jesus, I abhor these sins above every evil, and I unite my abhorrence of them to the abhorrence that You had for them in the garden of Gethsemane. I purpose, with Your grace, never more to offend You. My beloved Redeemer, give me a portion of that grief which You did feel for my sins in the garden of Gethsemane.

7. Jesus Himself, in enduring fears, weariness, and sorrows has merited for us a courage to resist the threats of those who would corrupt us, a strength to overcome the weariness we experience in prayer, in mortifications, and other

devout exercises, and a power of enduring with peace of mind that sadness which afflicts us in adversity. We must also know that He Himself in the garden, at the sight of all the pains and the desolate death that He was about to endure, chose to suffer this human weakness. He prayed to His Divine Father that, if it were possible, the cup might pass from Him. But immediately He added, "Nevertheless, not as I will, but as You will." And for the whole time that He continued praying in the garden, He repeated the same prayer, "Your will be done." With those words, "Your will be done", Jesus Christ merited and obtained for us resignation in all adversity, and gained for His martyrs and confessors a strength to resist all the persecutions and torments of tyrants.

8. Knowing that Judas, along with the Jews and soldiers who came to capture Him, was at hand, the Redeemer, still bathed in the sweat of death, rises with a pallid countenance, but with a heart all on fire with love, and goes to meet His enemies. He does this in order to deliver Himself into their hands. On seeing them He said, "Whom do you seek?" Imagine, O my soul, that Jesus then said to you, "Tell Me whom do you seek?" Ah! My Lord, and Whom will I seek but You, Who have come from heaven on earth to seek after me, and save me from perdition?

9. Behold how Judas, arriving in the garden together with the soldiers, advances, embraces His Master, and kisses Him. Jesus suffers him to kiss Him; but, knowing already his evil intent, could not refrain from complaining of this most unjust treachery, saying, "Judas, do You betray the Son of Man with a kiss?" Then those insolent servants crowd

around Jesus, lay hands upon Him, and bind Him as a villain. Oh my! what do I see? A God bound! By whom? By men; by worms created by Himself. Angels of paradise, what do you say to it? And You, my Jesus, why do You allow Yourself to be bound? What have the bonds of slaves and of the guilty to do with You, Who are the Holy of Holies, the King of kings, and Lord of lords? But if men bind You, why do You not loosen and free Yourself from the torments and death which they are preparing for You? But I understand this. It is not, O my Lord, these ropes which bind You. It is only love which keeps You bound, and constrains You to suffer and die for us. O Charity, how strong is Your chain, by which God was able to be bound! O divine Love, You were able to bind a God, and conduct Him to death for the love of men.

10. O Lord of the world, You are the greatest of all kings; but You have willed to be despised more than all men, in order to teach me the love of contempt. Because, then, You have sacrificed Your honour for love of me, I am willing to suffer for love of You every affront which shall be offered to me. And what kind of affronts did not the Redeemer suffer in His Passion? He saw Himself affronted by His own disciples. One of them betrays Him, and sells Him for thirty pieces. Another denies Him many times, protesting publicly that he knows Him not; and thus attesting that he was ashamed to have known Him in the past. The other disciples, then, at seeing Him taken and bound, all fly and abandon Him. O my Jesus, thus abandoned, who will ever undertake Your defence, if, when You are first taken, those most dear to You depart from and forsake You? But, my

God, to think that this dishonour did not end with Your Passion! How many souls, after having devoted themselves to follow You, and after having been favoured by You with many graces and special signs of love, being then driven by some passion of vile interest, or human respect, or sordid pleasure, have ungratefully forsaken You!

GLORY BE TO THE FATHER Glory be to the Father, and to the Son, and to the Holy Spirit, as it was in the beginning, is now and ever shall be, world without end. Amen.

THE FATIMA PRAYER O my Jesus, forgive us our sins, save us from the fires of hell, lead all souls to heaven, especially those in most need of Thy mercy.

The Scourging at the Pillar

THE FRUIT OF THIS MYSTERY

A deeper realisation that it was my sins that scourged our Lord's holy flesh

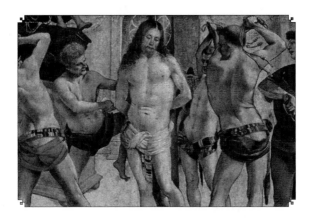

ET US ENTER INTO the praetorium of Pilate, one
day made the horrible scene of the ignominies and
pains of Jesus: let us see how unjust, how shameful,
how cruel, was the punishment there inflicted on the Saviour
of the world. Pilate, seeing that the Jews continued to make
a tumult against Jesus, as a most unjust judge condemned
Him to be scourged. The iniquitous judge thought by means

of this barbarity to win for Him the compassion of His enemies, and thus to deliver Him from death. Scourging was
the chastisement inflicted on slaves only. Therefore, it can
be said, that our loving Redeemer willed to take the form,
not only of a slave, in order to subject Himself to the will
of others, but even of a bad slave in order to be chastised
with scourges, and so to pay the penalty due from man,
who had made himself the slave of sin. A God scourged!
It is a greater marvel that God should receive the lightest
blow than for all men and all angels to be destroyed in an
instant. Ah, my Jesus, pardon me the offences that I have
committed against You, and then chastise me as shall please
You. This alone is enough, that I love You, and that You love
me; and then I am content to suffer all the pains You will.

OUR FATHER   Our Father, Who art in Heaven, hallowed
be Thy name, Thy kingdom come, Thy will be done, on
earth as it is in heaven. Give us this day our daily bread; and
forgive us our trespasses, as we forgive those who trespass
against us; and lead us not into temptation, but deliver us
from evil. Amen.

HAIL MARY (10)   Hail Mary, Full of Grace, the Lord is
with thee. Blessed art thou among women and blessed is
the fruit of thy womb, Jesus. Holy Mary, Mother of God,
pray for us sinners now, and at the hour of our death. Amen.

1. Look, O man, at these dogs dragging Him along, and the
Lamb, like a victim, meekly following without resistance.
One seizes, another binds Him; another drives, another
strikes Him. They carry our sweet Saviour, thus bound, first

to the house of Annas, then to that of Caiaphas; where Jesus, being asked by that wicked one about His disciples and His doctrine, replied that He had not spoken in private, but in public, and that they who were standing round about well knew what He had taught. But at this answer one of those servants, treating Him as if too bold, gave Him a blow on the cheek. Here exclaims St. Jerome, "You angels, how is it that you are silent? How long can such patience withhold you in your astonishment?" Ah, my Jesus, how could an answer so just and modest deserve such an affront in the presence of so many people? The worthless high-priest, instead of reproving the insolence of this audacious man, praises him, or at least by signs approves. And You, my Lord, suffered all this to compensate for the affronts which I, a wretch, have offered to the Divine Majesty by my sins. My Jesus, I thank You for it. Eternal Father, pardon me by the merits of Jesus.

2. Then the iniquitous high-priest asked Him if He were truly the Son of God. Jesus, out of respect for the name of God, affirmed that He was so indeed; whereupon Caiaphas rent his garments, saying that He had blasphemed; and all cried out that He deserved death. And then the rabble set themselves to ill-treat Him all the night through with blows, punches, kicks, and even spitting in His face, and mocking Him as a false prophet. All the pains and infirmities which Jesus suffered on that night will only be made known on the day of the last judgment. Ah, my Jesus, how is it that You are so humble and I am so proud? O Lord, give me light, make me know Who You are, and who I am. "Then they spat in His face." O God, what greater affront can there be

than to be defiled by spitting? Behold how these wretches outrage You and You do not threaten nor reprove them. No, like an innocent lamb, humble and meek, You suffered all without so much as complaining, offering all to the Father to obtain the pardon of our sins. If this medicine cannot cure our pride, I do not know what can.

3. When it was day, the Jews conduct Jesus to Pilate, to make him condemn Him to death; but Pilate declares Him to be innocent. And to free himself from the importunities of the Jews who pressed on him, seeking the death of the Saviour, he sends Him to Herod. It greatly pleased Herod to see Jesus Christ brought before him, hoping that in his presence, in order to deliver Himself from death, He would have worked one of those miracles of which he had heard tell; wherefore he asked Him many questions. But Jesus, because He did not wish to be delivered from death, and because that wicked one was not worthy of His answers, was silent, and answered him not. Then the proud king, with his court, offered Him many insults, and making them cover Him with a white robe, as if declaring Him to be ignorant and stupid, sent Him back to Pilate. O Eternal Wisdom, O Divine Word! This one other ignominy was wanting to You, that You should be treated as a fool bereft of sense. So greatly does our salvation weigh on You, that through love of us You will not only to be reviled, but to be satiated with reviling. And how could You bear such love to men, from whom You have received nothing but ingratitude and slights? Alas, that I should be one of these who have outraged You worse than Herod! Ah, my Jesus, chastise me not, like Herod, by depriving me of Your voice. Herod did not recognise

You for what You are; I confess You to be my God. Herod loved You not; I love You more than myself. Deny me not I beseech You, deny me not the voice of Your inspiration, as I have deserved by the offences that I have committed against You. Tell me what You will have of me, for, by Your grace, I am ready to do all that You will.

4. As soon as He had arrived at the praetorium, our loving Saviour, at the command of the servants, stripped Himself of his garments, embraced the column, and then laid on it His hands to have them bound. O God, already is begun the cruel torture! O angels of heaven, come and look on this sorrowful spectacle; and if it be not permitted you to deliver your king from this barbarous slaughter which men have prepared for Him, at least come and weep for compassion. And you, my soul, imagine yourself to be present at this horrible tearing of the flesh of Your beloved Redeemer. Look on Him, how He stands, Your afflicted Jesus, with His head bowed looking on the ground, blushing all over for shame, He awaits this great torture. Behold these barbarians, like so many ravenous dogs, are already with the scourges attacking this innocent lamb. See how one beats Him on the breast, another strikes His shoulders, another smites His back and His legs; even His sacred head and His beautiful face cannot escape the blows. His divine blood flows from every part; the scourges, the hands of the executioners, the column, the ground, they are all saturated with that blood. Ah, cruel men, with Whom are you dealing thus? Know that you are mistaken. This man Whom you are torturing is innocent and holy; it is I who am the culprit; to me, to me, to the one who has sinned, are these stripes and torments due.

5. "Behold the Lamb of God"; thus did the Baptist speak of our Blessed Redeemer, Who offered His blood and even His life in sacrifice to obtain our pardon and our eternal salvation. Behold Him in the hall of Pilate; as an innocent Lamb He permits Himself to be shorn, not of wool, but of His sacred flesh, with thorns and scourges. He opens not His mouth, nor does He complain, because He desires to suffer Himself the punishments due to our sins. May the angels and all creatures bless You, O Saviour of the world, for the great mercy and love which You have shown towards us. We committed sins, and You made satisfaction for them.

6. "I well know", says the Eternal Father, "that this My son is innocent; but inasmuch as He has offered Himself as a satisfaction to My justice for all the sins of mankind, it is fitting that I should so abandon Him to the rage of His enemies." Have You, then, my adorable Saviour, in compensation for our sins, and especially for those of impurity, that most prevalent vice of mankind, been willing to have Your most pure flesh torn in pieces? And who, then, will not exclaim, "How unspeakable is the love of the Son of God towards sinners!" Ah, my Lord, smitten with the scourge, I return You thanks for so great love, and I grieve that I am myself, by reason of my sins, one of those who scourge You. O my Jesus! I detest all those wicked pleasures which have cost You so much pain. Oh, how many years ought I not already to have been in the flames of hell! And why have You so patiently awaited me until now? You have borne with me, in order that at length, overcome by so many wiles of love, I might give myself up to love You, abandoning sin.

7. The divine blood was issuing from every pore; the sacred body had become but one perfect wound; yet those infuriated brutes continued to add blow to blow, as the Prophet had foretold, "And they have added to the grief of My wounds." So that the strokes of the whip not only made the whole body one wound, but even bore away pieces of it into the air, until at length the gashes in that sacred flesh were such that the bones might have been counted. Jesus Christ ought, naturally speaking, to have died; but He willed, by His divine power, to keep Himself in life, in order to suffer yet greater pains for love of us. Oh, what place in hell should there not be set apart for me, if, after having known the love that You have borne towards such a wretch, I should damn myself, despising a God Who had suffered scorn, smitings, and scourgings for me.

8. Cruel in excess to our Redeemer was this torture of His scourging. In the first place, because of the great number of those by whom it was inflicted; who, as was revealed to St. Mary Magdalen of Pazzi, were not fewer than sixty men. And these, at the instigation of the devils, and even more so of the Jewish priests, aimed at taking away His life by means of this scourging, lest Pilate release Him afterwards. The sharpest implements were selected by these wicked men, so that every stroke produced a wound and thus the number amounted to several thousand. Our Lord revealed Himself to St. Teresa in the time of His scourging, in which large pieces of His flesh were torn off, hanging down from the left elbow. Ah, my beloved and adored Jesus, how much have You suffered for love of me! Oh, let not so many pangs, and so much blood, be lost for me!

9. Jesus one day manifested Himself under His scourging to Sister Victoria Angelini; and showing her His body one mass of wounds, said to her, "These wounds, Victoria, every one of them, ask you for love." Yes, my sweet Saviour, I see You all covered with wounds; I look into Your beautiful face; but, O my God, it no longer wears its beautiful appearance, but disfigured and blackened with blood, and bruises, and shameful spittings. But the more I see You so disfigured, O my Lord, the more beautiful and lovely You appear to me. And what are these disfigurements that I behold but signs of the tenderness of that love which You bear towards me? I love You, my Jesus, thus wounded and torn to pieces for me; would that I could see myself too torn to pieces for You, like so many martyrs whose portion this has been! But if I cannot offer You wounds and blood, I offer You at least all the pains which it will be my lot to suffer. I offer You my heart; with this I desire to love You more tenderly even than I am able. And who is there that my soul should love more tenderly than a God, who has endured scourging and been drained of His blood for me?

10. He who lives to the world seeks to please the world; he who lives to himself seeks to please himself; but he who lives to Jesus Christ seeks only to please Jesus Christ, and fears only to displease Him. His only joy is to see Him loved; his only sorrow, to see Him despised. This is to live for Jesus Christ; and this is what He claims from each one of us. I repeat, does He claim too much from us, after having given us His blood and His life? Why, then, O my God! Do we employ our affections in loving creatures, relatives, friends, the great ones of the world, who have never suffered for

us scourges, thorns, or nails, nor shed one drop of blood for us; and not in loving a God, who for love of us came down from heaven and was made man, and has shed all His blood for us in the midst of torments, in order to win to Himself our hearts!

GLORY BE TO THE FATHER   Glory be to the Father, and to the Son, and to the Holy Spirit, as it was in the beginning, is now and ever shall be, world without end. Amen.

THE FATIMA PRAYER   O my Jesus, forgive us our sins, save us from the fires of hell, lead all souls to heaven, especially those in most need of Thy mercy.

The Crowning with Thorns

THE FRUIT OF THIS MYSTERY

To remain faithful to Christ in times of trial

"HAIL, KING OF THE Jews." Thus was our Redeemer scornfully saluted by the Roman soldiers. After having treated Him as a false king, and having crowned Him with thorns, they knelt before Him and called Him king of the Jews, and then, rising up with loud cries and laughter, they struck Him and spat in His face. O my Jesus! This barbarous crown that encircles Your head, this vile reed that You hold in Your hand, this torn purple garment that covers You with ridicule, all these make You known indeed as a king, but a king of love. My beloved Redeemer, if others will not have You for their king, I accept You, and desire that You should be the only King of my soul. To You do I consecrate my whole self; dispose of me as You please. For this end have You endured contempt, so many sorrows, and death itself, to gain our hearts and to reign therein by Your love. Make Yourself, therefore, master of my heart, O my beloved King, and reign and exercise Your sway there forever. Formerly I refused You for my Lord, that I might serve my passions; now I will be all Yours and You alone will I serve. Ah, bind me to You by Your love, and make me always remember the bitter death that You have willed to suffer for me. Ah, my King, my God, my love, my all, what do I wish for if not for You alone!

OUR FATHER   Our Father, Who art in Heaven, hallowed be Thy name, Thy kingdom come, Thy will be done, on earth as it is in heaven. Give us this day our daily bread; and forgive us our trespasses, as we forgive those who trespass against us; and lead us not into temptation, but deliver us from evil. Amen.

HAIL MARY (10)   Hail Mary, Full of Grace, the Lord is with thee. Blessed art thou among women and blessed is the fruit of thy womb, Jesus. Holy Mary, Mother of God, pray for us sinners now, and at the hour of our death. Amen.

1. As the soldiers, however, perseveringly continued their cruel scourging of the innocent Lamb, it is related that one

of those who was standing by came forward, and, taking courage, said to them, "You have no orders to kill this man, as you are trying to do." And, saying this, he cut the cords wherewith the Lord was standing bound. But hardly was the scourging ended, when those barbarous men, urged on and bribed by the Jews inflict upon the Redeemer a fresh kind of torture. Behold how the soldiers strip Him again; and, treating Him as a mock king, place upon Him a purple garment, which was nothing else but a ragged cloak, one of those that were worn by the Roman soldiers. And in His hand they place a reed to represent a sceptre, and upon His head a bundle of thorns to represent a crown.

2. Ah, my Jesus, and are not You, then, true king of the universe? And how is it that You are now become king of sorrow and reproach? See to where love has brought You! O my most loving God, when will that day arrive whereon I may so unite myself to You, that nothing may evermore have power to separate me from You, and I may no longer be able to cease to love You!

3. "And plating a crown of thorns, they put it upon His head." This torture of the crown of thorns was one most full of pain; inasmuch as they everywhere pierced into the sacred head of the Lord, the most sensitive part, it being from the head that all the nerves and sensations of the body diverge. It was also that torture of His Passion which lasted the longest, as Jesus suffered from the thorns up to His death, remaining, as they did, fixed in His head. Every time that the thorns on His head were touched, the anguish was renewed afresh. The crown was intertwined with several

branches of thorns, and fashioned like a helmet or hat, so that it fitted upon the whole of the head, down to the middle of the forehead; The thorns were so long that they penetrated even to the brain.

4. While the gentle Lamb let Himself be tormented, according to the will of the soldiers, He did not speak a word, He did not cry out, but, compressing His eyes together through the anguish, He frequently breathed forth bitter sighs, as occurs in someone undergoing a torture which has brought him to the point of death. So great was the quantity of the blood which flowed from the wounds upon His sacred head, that upon His face there was no appearance of any other colour save that of blood. So many streams of blood rushing down over His face, and filling His hair, and eyes, and beard, He seemed to be nothing but one mass of blood. The beautiful face of the Lord was no longer seen, but it appeared rather the face of a man of a leper.

5. On one occasion when Our Lord appeared to St. Teresa crowned with thorns, the saint began to compassionate Him; but the Lord made answer to her, "Teresa, compassionate Me not on account of the wounds which the thorns of the Jews produced; but commiserate Me on account of the wounds which the sins of Christians occasion Me." You, too, therefore, O my soul, did then inflict torture upon the venerable head of your Redeemer by so often consenting to evil. Open now your eyes, and see, and bitterly bewail all your life long the evil that you have

done in so ungratefully turning your back upon your Lord and God.

6. When those barbarians had placed upon the head of Jesus that crown of torture, it was not enough for them to press it down as forcibly as they could with their hands, but they took a reed to answer the purpose of a hammer, that so they might make the thorns penetrate the more deeply. They then began to turn Him into derision, as if He had been a mock king; first of all saluting Him on their bended knee as King of the Jews; and then, rising up, they spit into His face, and buffeted Him with shouts and jests of scorn. Ah, my Jesus, to what are You reduced! Had any one happened by chance to pass that place and seen Jesus Christ so drained of blood, clad in that ragged purple garment, with that sceptre in His hand, with that crown upon His head, and so derided and ill-treated by that low rabble, what would He ever have taken Him to be but the vilest and most wicked man in the world! Behold the Son of God become at that time the disgrace of Jerusalem! "O men", hereupon exclaims the Blessed Denis, the Carthusian, "if we will not love Jesus Christ because He is good, because He is God, let us love him at least for the many pains which He has suffered for us."

7. When Jesus was brought before Pilate after the scourging and crowning with thorns, Pilate looked at Him, and seeing him so mangled and deformed, felt persuaded that He would move the people to compassion by merely exposing Him to their view. Hence he went forth to the balcony, bringing with him our afflicted Saviour, and said to the people,

"Behold the man"; as if he said, "O Jews, be content with what this innocent man has already suffered. Behold the man; behold the man Whom you suspected of wishing to become your king: behold Him, see the miserable condition to which He is reduced. What fear can you now have of Him, when it is impossible for Him to recover from His wounds? Let Him go and die in His own house; He has but a short time to live. Behold your king now reduced to such a state that He wears the appearance of a man that has been flayed alive; and He can have but little life left in Him. If, with all this, you want me to condemn Him to death, I tell you that I cannot do so, as I find not any reason for condemning Him." But the Jews on beholding Jesus thus ill-treated, waxed more fierce, "When, therefore, the chief priests and the officers saw Him, they cried out, saying, 'Crucify Him! Crucify Him!'"

8. But while Pilate from the balcony was exhibiting Jesus to that populace, at the self-same time the Eternal Father from heaven was presenting to us His beloved son, saying, in like manner, "Behold the man." "Behold this man, Who is My only-begotten son, Whom I love with the same love wherewith I love Myself. Behold the man, your Saviour, Him Whom I promised, and for Whom you were anxiously waiting. Behold the man, Who is nobler than all other men, become the man of sorrows. Behold Him, and see to what a pitiable condition He has reduced Himself through the love which He has borne towards you, and in order to be, at least out of compassion, beloved by you again. Oh, look at Him, and love Him." Ah, my God and Father of my Redeemer! I love Your son, Who suffers for love of me; and I love You,

Who with so much love have abandoned Him to so many pains for me. Oh, look not on my sins by which I have so often offended You and Your son, rather "Look upon the face of Your Christ." Behold Your only-begotten, all covered with wounds and shame in satisfaction for my faults; and for His merits pardon me, and never let me again offend You.

9. Pilate, the governor, inquired of the people whom they wished to have released at that Passover, Jesus or Barabbas. But the people cried out, "Not this Man, but Barabbas." Then said Pilate, "What, then, shall I do with Jesus?" They answered, "Let Him be crucified." "But what evil has this innocent one done?" replied Pilate. They repeated, "Let Him be crucified." And even up to this time, O God, the greater part of mankind continue to say, "Not this Man, but Barabbas", preferring to Jesus Christ some pleasure of sense, some point of honour, some outbreak of wounded pride. Ah, my Lord, well know You that at one time I did You the same injury when I preferred my accursed tastes to You. My Jesus, pardon me, for I repent of the past, and henceforth I prefer You before everything. I esteem You, I love You more than any good; and am willing a thousand times to die rather than forsake You. Give me holy perseverance; give me Your love.

10. Pilate said to the Jews, "Shall I crucify your King?" and they made answer, "We have no king but Caesar." The worldly-minded, who love the riches, the honours, and the pleasures of earth, refuse to have Jesus Christ for their king; because, as far as this earth is concerned, Jesus was but a king of poverty, shame, and sufferings. But if such as these

refuse You, O my Jesus, we choose You for our only king, and we make our protestation that "we have no king but Jesus." Yes, most lovely Saviour, You are my king; You are and have forever to be my only Lord. True king, indeed, are You of our souls; for You have created them, and redeemed them from the slavery of Satan. Exercise, then, Your dominion, and reign forever in our poor hearts; may they ever serve and obey You! Be it for others to serve the monarchs of earth, in hope of the good things of this world. Our desire it is to serve only You, our afflicted and despised king, in hope only of pleasing You, without any earthly consolations. Grant us only that which Your faithful and loving servant St. John of the Cross asked of You, "Lord, to suffer and be despised for You; Lord, to suffer and be despised for You!"

GLORY BE TO THE FATHER   Glory be to the Father, and to the Son, and to the Holy Spirit, as it was in the beginning, is now and ever shall be, world without end. Amen.

THE FATIMA PRAYER   O my Jesus, forgive us our sins, save us from the fires of hell, lead all souls to heaven, especially those in most need of Thy mercy.

The Carrying of the Cross

THE FRUIT OF THIS MYSTERY

Resignation and patience in all the tribulations of life

HE CROSS BEGAN TO torture Jesus Christ before He was nailed upon it; for after He was condemned by Pilate, the cross on which He was to die was given to Him to carry to Calvary, and, without refusing, He took it upon His shoulders. Speaking of this, St. Augustine writes, "If we regard the wickedness of His tormentors, the insult was great; if we regard the love of Jesus, the mystery

77

is great; for in carrying the cross, our Captain then lifted up the standard under which His followers upon this earth must be enrolled and must fight, in order to be made His companions in the Kingdom of Heaven." St. Basil, speaking of the passage in Isaiah, "A child is born to us, and a son is given to us, and the government is upon His shoulder" remarks, "The kings of the earth found their sovereignties in the force of arms and in the heaping-up of riches; but Jesus Christ founded His sovereignty in the insults of the cross", that is, in humbling Himself and in suffering, and on this account He willingly accepted the cross, and carried it on that painful journey, in order, by His example, to give us courage to embrace with resignation every cross, and thus to follow Him. Wherefore, also, He said to His disciples, "If any man will come after Me, let him deny himself, and take up his cross and follow Me."

OUR FATHER   Our Father, Who art in Heaven, hallowed be Thy name, Thy kingdom come, Thy will be done, on earth as it is in heaven. Give us this day our daily bread; and forgive us our trespasses, as we forgive those who trespass against us; and lead us not into temptation, but deliver us from evil. Amen.

HAIL MARY (10)   Hail Mary, Full of Grace, the Lord is with thee. Blessed art thou among women and blessed is the fruit of thy womb, Jesus. Holy Mary, Mother of God, pray for us sinners now, and at the hour of our death. Amen.

1. Morning having arrived, the disciples of Jesus Christ came to the afflicted mother. One came to relate to her the cruel

treatment of her son in the house of Caiaphas; another, the insults received by Him from Herod. Finally, St. John came and announced to Mary that the most unjust Pilate had already condemned Him to death upon the cross. I say the most unjust, for, this unjust judge condemned Him to death with the same lips with which he had pronounced Him innocent. "Ah, sorrowful mother"; said St. John to her, "Your son has already been condemned to death, He is already on His way, bearing Himself His cross on His way to Calvary. Come, if you desire to see Him, and bid Him a last farewell in some of the streets through which He is to pass."

2. As soon as the sentence is proclaimed, those faithless Jews gathered in the praetorium raise a shout of exultation, and say, "Rejoice, rejoice; Jesus is already condemned. Make haste, lose no time; prepare the cross, and put Him to death before tomorrow which will be the Paschal solemnity." They instantly seize Him; tear off the scarlet cloak, and put on His own clothes, that He might be recognised by the people as the one they now considered as an impostor, Whom they had a few days before hailed as the Messiah. They then take two large beams, make a cross, and insolently command Him to carry it on His shoulders to the place of His execution. O God! what barbarity! To put so heavy a burden on a man who has been so tortured and exhausted of strength.

3. Mary goes with St. John, and she perceives by the blood with which the way was sprinkled, that her son had already passed there. This she revealed to St. Bridget, "By the footsteps of my son I traced His course, for along the way

by which He had passed, the ground was sprinkled with blood." She places herself at the corner of a street to meet her afflicted son as He passes by, and thus this most afflicted mother met her most afflicted son. While Mary stopped and waited His passing how much she must have heard said against her son by the Jews who knew her, and perhaps also words in mockery of herself! Alas! What a commencement of sorrows was then before her eyes, when she saw the nails, the hammers, the cords, the fatal instruments of the death of her son borne before Him! And what a sword pierced her heart when she heard the trumpet proclaiming along the way the sentence pronounced against her son! But behold, now, after the instruments, the trumpet, and the ministers of justice had passed, she raises her eyes and sees; she sees, oh God, a young man covered with blood and wounds from head to foot, with a crown of thorns on His head, and two heavy beams on His shoulders; she looks at Him and hardly knows Him, yes, for the wounds, the bruises, and clotted blood, made Him look like a leper, so that He could no longer be recognised. But at length love recognises Him, and as soon as she knows Him, they look at each other. The son wipes from His eyes the clotted blood, which prevented Him from seeing, and looks upon the mother; the mother looks upon the Son. Ah, looks of sorrow, which pierced, as with so many arrows, those two holy and loving souls. When Margaret, the daughter of St. Thomas More, met her father on his way to the scaffold, she could utter only two words, "Oh, father! oh, father!" and fell fainting at his feet. At the sight of her son going to Calvary, Mary fainted not; but if she did not die, she suffered sorrow enough to cause her a thousand deaths.

4. The mother wished to embrace Him, but the officers of justice thrust her aside, loading her with insults, and urge onward our afflicted Lord. Mary follows. Ah, holy Virgin, where are you going? To Calvary! And can you trust yourself to see Him who is your life hanging from a cross? And your life shall be as it were hanging before you. Our Lord would ask, "Ah! My mother, where do you hasten? Where are you going? If you come where I go, you will be tortured with My sufferings, and I with yours." But although the sight of her dying Jesus must cost her such cruel anguish, the loving Mary will not leave Him. The son goes before, and the mother follows, that she may be crucified with her son. We even pity the wild beasts, If we should see a lioness following her whelp as he was led to death, even this wild beast would call forth our compassion. And shall we not feel compassion to see Mary following her immaculate Lamb, as they are leading Him to death? Let us then pity her, and endeavour also ourselves to accompany her son and herself, bearing with patience the cross which the Lord imposes upon us.

5. Jesus refuses not the cross; with love He embraces it, as being the altar whereon is destined to be completed the sacrifice of His life for the salvation of men. The condemned criminals now come forth from Pilate's residence, and in the midst of them there goes also our condemned Lord. O that sight, which filled both heaven and earth with amazement! To see the Son of God going to die for the sake of those very men from whose hands He is receiving His death! Behold the prophecy fulfilled, "And I was as a meek lamb, that is carried to be a victim." The appearance that Jesus made

on this journey was so pitiable that the Jewish women, on beholding Him, followed Him in tears.

6. Behold my soul, now that your condemned Saviour is passing, behold how He moves along, dripping with blood that keeps flowing from His still fresh wounds, crowned with thorns, and laden with the cross. Alas, how at every motion is the pain of all His wounds renewed! The cross, from the first moment, begins its torture, pressing heavily upon His wounded shoulders, and cruelly acting like a hammer upon the thorns of the crown. O God! At every step, how great are the sufferings!

7. Look at Him, O my soul, see Him moving along with His flesh all torn, carrying a crown of thorns on His head and a heavy cross on His shoulders, surrounded by enemies who load Him with insults and maledictions. O God! His sacred body is all mangled, so that at every step the pain of His wounds is renewed. The cross torments Him before He is fastened to it, for it presses on His wounded shoulders, and cruelly beats into His head the thorns of that barbarous crown. Alas, how great and manifold His pain at every step! But Jesus leaves not the cross; no, He does not leave it, because through it He wishes to reign in the hearts of men. Ah, my Jesus, with what sentiments of love for me did You then go to Calvary, where You were to consummate the great sacrifice of Your life! My soul, embrace your cross for the love of Jesus, Who suffers so much for your sake. See how He goes before with His cross, and invites you to follow Him with yours, "If any man will come after Me, let him take up his cross and follow Me." My Jesus, I do not wish

to leave You; I wish to follow You till death; but, through the merits of this painful journey, give me strength to carry with patience the crosses which You send me.

8. "Love is patient," says St. Paul, "it bears all things." It patiently carries the external as well as the internal crosses; the loss of health, of fortune, of honour, of relatives and friends; anguish, temptations, pains and spiritual aridity. By patience virtue is tried. On this account such stress is laid, in the lives of the saints, on their patience in contradictions. The devil tempts us to try our patience, "Because You were acceptable to God, it was necessary that temptation should prove you." When the Lord gives one an occasion of suffering much, a heavy cross, He shows a greater love for such a one than if He gave him the power to raise the dead to life; for when we work miracles we are debtors to God, but when we suffer patiently, God becomes, so to say, a debtor to us. Whether we will it or not, we must all bear the sufferings that God's Providence has allotted to us. It is to our advantage, therefore, to suffer with merit, and that means to suffer with patience. Ask God earnestly for this precious gift, the grace to suffer the trials and tribulations of life with patience and conformity to His holy will.

9. O Lord, I am a pilgrim upon this earth; teach me to keep Your precepts, which are the road by which I may reach my country in Heaven. It is not surprising that the wicked should wish to live forever in this world, for they justly fear that they will pass from the pains of this life to the eternal and far more terrible pains of Hell; but how can he who loves God, and has a moral certainty that he is in

the state of grace, desire to go on living in this vale of tears in continual bitterness, in anxieties of conscience, in peril of being condemned? How can he not sigh to depart speedily to unite himself to God in a blessed eternity, where there is no longer any danger of losing Him? He that runs in a race pays no heed to the spectators, but only to the crown of victory; he stops not, but the nearer he approaches the goal, the quicker he runs. Therefore, the longer we have lived, the more we should hasten by good works to secure the prize. Behold, O my God, my heart is ready; behold me prepared for every cross which You shall send me.

10. As soon as Jesus arrived at Calvary, oppressed with pain and fatigue, they gave Him to drink wine mixed with gall, which was ordinarily given to persons condemned to the death of the cross, in order to diminish their sensibility to pain. But because Jesus wished to die without comfort, He tasted, but would not drink it. The people therefore formed a circle round Jesus; the soldiers took off His garments, which, because they were fastened to His wounded and mangled body, took with them pieces of flesh. They then threw Him on the cross. Jesus stretched out His sacred hands, offered to the Eternal Father the great sacrifice of Himself, and prayed Him to accept it for our salvation.

GLORY BE TO THE FATHER   Glory be to the Father, and to the Son, and to the Holy Spirit, as it was in the beginning, is now and ever shall be, world without end. Amen.

THE FATIMA PRAYER   O my Jesus, forgive us our sins, save us from the fires of hell, lead all souls to heaven, especially those in most need of Thy mercy.

The Crucifixion of Our Lord

THE FRUIT OF THIS MYSTERY

To think often of the love of Jesus Christ for me, in dying for me

J ESUS UPON THE CROSS was a spectacle which filled heaven and earth with amazement, at the sight of Almighty God, the Lord of all, dying upon an infamous gibbet, condemned as a malefactor between two other malefactors. It was a spectacle of justice, It was a spectacle of mercy. Most of all it was a spectacle of love, in displaying a God who offered and gave His life to redeem from death His slaves and enemies. Comforted by the sight of Jesus derided upon the cross, the saints have loved contempt more than worldly people have loved all the honours of the world. At the sight of Jesus naked and dying upon the cross, they have sought to abandon all the good things of this earth. At the sight of Him all wounded upon the cross, while the blood flowed forth from all His limbs, they have learnt to abhor sensual pleasures, and have sought to afflict their flesh as much as they could, in order to accompany with their own sufferings the sufferings of the Crucified. It is this spectacle which ever was and ever will be the dearest object of the contemplations of the saints, through which they have counted it little to strip themselves of all earthly pleasures and goods, and to embrace with desire and joy both pain and death, in order to make some return of gratitude to a God Who died for love of them.

OUR FATHER   Our Father, Who art in Heaven, hallowed be Thy name, Thy kingdom come, Thy will be done, on earth as it is in heaven. Give us this day our daily bread; and forgive us our trespasses, as we forgive those who trespass against us; and lead us not into temptation, but deliver us from evil. Amen.

HAIL MARY (10)   Hail Mary, Full of Grace, the Lord is with thee. Blessed art thou among women and blessed is the fruit of thy womb, Jesus. Holy Mary, Mother of God, pray for us sinners now, and at the hour of our death. Amen.

1. Behold they took the nails and hammers, and piercing the hands and feet of the Saviour, they fastened Him to

the cross. The noise of the hammers resounded through the mountains, and was heard by Mary, who followed her son, and had already arrived at the place of execution. O sacred hands, which by Your touch have healed so many sick, why are You now pierced on this cross? O sacred feet, so often wearied in seeking after lost sheep, why are You now transfixed with nails? Why do You suffer so intense a pain? When a nerve is punctured, the pain is so acute that it causes the swoons and spasms of death. How great, then, must have been the pain which Jesus suffered when His hands and feet, parts of the body which are full of bones and nerves, were pierced with the nails? Behold the cross is raised along with Jesus Christ Who is fastened to it, and is let fall with violence into the hole prepared for it. It is then made fast in its place, and Our Blessed Lord hangs between two thieves.

2. Jesus on the cross! Behold the proof of the love of a God. Behold the last appearance of the Incarnate Word on earth. The first was in a stable, the last is on a cross: both display His love and infinite charity for men. Contemplating one day the love of Jesus in dying for us, St. Francis of Paul, wrapt in ecstasy and raised in the air, exclaimed three times, in a loud voice, "O God, love! O God, love! O God, love!" By these exclamations the Lord wished, through the saint, to teach us that we shall never be able to comprehend the infinite love which this God has shown us in condescending to suffer such torments, and to die for our salvation. My soul, approach with a humbled and penitent heart that cross; kiss the altar on which Your loving Lord dies. Place yourself under His feet, that His divine blood may flow

upon you, and say to the Eternal Father, "May this blood descend on us, and wash us from our sins, this blood does not demand vengeance from You, as did the blood of Abel, but implores of You for us mercy and pardon."

3. We observe that the Queen of Martyrs endures a sort of martyrdom more cruel than any other martyrdom, that of a mother so placed as to behold an innocent son executed upon a gibbet of infamy. Ever since Jesus was apprehended in the garden, He has been abandoned by His disciples; but Mary abandons Him not. She stays with Him till she sees Him expire before her eyes, "She stood close by." Mothers, in general, flee away from the presence of their sons when they see them suffer, and cannot render them any assistance: content enough would they be themselves to endure their sons' sufferings; and, therefore, when they see them suffering without the power of succouring them, they have not the strength to endure so great a pain, and consequently flee away, and go to a distance. Not so Mary. She sees her son in torments; she sees that the pains are taking His life away; but she flees not, nor moves to a distance. On the contrary, she draws near to the cross whereon her son is dying. O sorrowing Mary! disdain me not for a companion to assist at the death of your Jesus and mine.

4. Behold how the loving Saviour is now drawing nigh to death. Behold, O my soul, those beautiful eyes growing dim, that face become all pallid, that heart all but ceasing to beat, and that sacred body now disposing itself to the final surrender of its life. After Jesus had received the vinegar, He said, "It is consummated". He then passed over in review before

His eyes all the sufferings that He had undergone during His life, in the shape of poverty, contempt, and pain; and then offering them all up to the Eternal Father, He turned to Him and said, "It is finished". "My Father, behold by the sacrifice of My death, the work of the world's redemption, which You have laid upon Me, is now completed." And it seems as through, turning Himself again to us, He repeated, "It is finished"; as if He would have said, "O men, O men, love Me, for I have done all; there is nothing more that I can do in order to gain your love."

5. Behold now, lastly, Jesus dies. Come, you angels of heaven, come and assist at the death of your King. And you, O sorrowing Mother Mary, draw nearer to the cross, and fix your eyes yet more attentively on your son, for He is now on the point of death. Behold Him, how, after having commended His spirit to His Eternal Father, He calls upon death, giving it permission to come to take away His life. "Come, O death", says He to it, "be quick and perform your office; slay Me, and save My flock." The earth now trembles, the graves open, the veil of the temple is rent in twain. The strength of the dying Saviour is failing through the violence of the sufferings; the warmth of His body is gradually diminishing; He gives up His body to death; He bows His head down upon His breast, He opens His mouth and dies. The people behold Him expire, and, observing that He no longer moves, they say, "He is dead, He is dead." He is dead! O God! Who is it that is dead? The author of life, the only-begotten Son of God, the Lord of the World, He is dead. O death of Christ, You were the amazement of heaven and of all nature. O infinite love! A God to sacrifice

His blood and His life! And for whom? For His ungrateful creatures; dying in an ocean of sufferings and shame, in order to pay the penalty due to their sins. Ah, infinite goodness! O infinite love! O my Jesus! You are, then, dead, on account of the love which You have borne me! Oh, let me never again live, even for a single moment, without loving You! I love You, my chief and only good; I love You, my Jesus, dead for me! O my sorrowing Mother Mary! Help a servant of yours, who desires to love Jesus.

6. Raise up your eyes, my soul, and behold that crucified man. Behold the divine Lamb now sacrificed upon that altar of pain. Consider that He is the beloved son of the Eternal Father; and consider that He is dead for the love that He has borne you. See how He holds His arms stretched out to embrace you; His head bent down to give the kiss of peace; His side open to receive you into His heart. Does not a God so loving deserve to be loved? Listen to the words He addresses to you from that cross, "Look, My son, and see whether there be any one in the world who has loved you more than I have." O my dear Redeemer! Well do I recognise in these Your wounds, and in Your lacerated body, as it were through so many lattices, the tender affection which You retain for me. Since, then, in order to pardon me, You have not pardoned Yourself, oh, look upon me now with the same love wherewith You did one day look upon me from the cross, whilst You were dying for me. Look upon me and enlighten me, and draw my whole heart to Yourself, that so, from this day forth, I may love none else but You. Let me not ever be unmindful of Your death. You promised that, when raised up upon the cross, You would draw all

hearts to Yourself. Behold this heart of mine, which, made tender by Your death, and enamoured of You, desires to offer no further resistance to Your calls. Oh, draw it to Yourself, and make it all Your own!

7. O God, had the vilest of all men suffered for me what Jesus Christ has suffered; had I beheld a man torn with scourges, fastened to a cross, and made the laughing-stock of the people in order to save my life, could I remember his sufferings without feeling for him the tenderest affection? And were the likeness of my expiring lover brought before me, could I behold it with indifference? Alas, how many Christians keep a beautiful crucifix in their room, but only as a fine piece of furniture! They praise the workmanship and the expression of grief, but it makes as little impression on their hearts as if it were not the image of the Incarnate Word, but of a man who was a stranger and unknown to them. Ah, my Jesus, do not permit me to be one of them. O sorrows of Jesus, O ignominies of Jesus, O death of Jesus, O love of Jesus! May You be fixed in my heart, and may the sweet remembrance of You remain there forever, to wound me continually, and to inflame me with love. Pardon particularly my past ingratitude to You, in thinking so little of Your Passion, and on the love You have shown me in Your sufferings.

8. The Jews wished the body of Jesus to be taken down from the cross; but because they could not take down a criminal until he was dead, they came with iron mallets to break His legs, as they had already done to the two thieves crucified with Him. And Mary, while she remains weeping at the

death of her son, sees those armed men coming towards her Jesus. At this sight she first trembled with fear, then she said, "My son is already dead, cease to maltreat Him, and cease to torture me, His poor mother, any longer." She implored them not to break His legs but while she is thus speaking, she sees a soldier with violence brandishing a spear, and piercing the side of Jesus. The cross shook at the stroke of the spear, and the heart of Jesus was divided There came out blood and water. The injury of that stroke was offered to Jesus, but the pain was inflicted on Mary. This was the very sword predicted to the Virgin by St. Simeon; a sword, not of iron, but of grief, which pierced through her blessed soul in the heart of Jesus, where it always dwelt. The spear which opened His side passed through the soul of the Virgin, which could not be torn from the heart of Jesus.

9. It was revealed to St. Bridget, that to take down the body of Jesus, three ladders were placed against the cross. The afflicted mother raised herself, and extending her arms to meet her dear son embraces Him, and then sits with Him at the foot of the cross. She sees His mouth open, His eyes shut, she examines the lacerated flesh, the exposed bones; she takes off the crown, and sees the cruel injury made by the thorns in His sacred head; she looks upon those pierced hands and feet, and says, "Ah, my son, to what has the love You did bear to men reduce you! But what evil have You done to them, that they have treated you so cruelly? You were my father, my brother, my spouse, my delight, my glory, my all." Then turning to those barbarous instruments, she said, "Oh cruel thorns, oh nails, oh merciless spear, how could you thus torture your Creator? No, it was not you, but

sinners, who cruelly treated my son." Thus Mary spoke and complained of us. But if now she were capable of suffering, what would she say? What grief would she feel to see that men after the death of her son, continue to torment and crucify Him by their sins? Let us no longer give pain to this sorrowful mother; and if we also have hitherto grieved her by our sins, let us now do as she directs. She says to us, "Return, you transgressors, to the heart, sinners, return to the wounded heart of my Jesus; return as penitents, for He will receive you. My son had wished His side to be opened that He might give you His heart, flee to Him then, and give Him your heart."

10. O my God! I offer You my life, and I am prepared to die at any hour that may be pleasing to Your holy will. "Your will be done", ever, ever, may Your will be done. O Lord! if You will to leave me in life for some time longer, blessed be Your name; but I desire not life, except to spend it all in loving You. If You will that I should die of a present sickness, still blessed are You. I embrace death to do Your will, and I repeat, "Your will, Your will be done;" I desire also to die, in order that, by the pain and bitterness of my death, I may satisfy Your divine justice for all my sins, through which I have offended You and deserved hell. I desire also to die, that I may nevermore offend You, or cause You displeasure in this life. I also desire to die in acknowledgment of the gratitude which I owe You for all the benefits and gifts that You have given me, contrary to what I deserve. I desire to die, that I may show that I love Your will more than my life. O my Jesus! You did accept the death of the cross through love of me; I accept death, and all the pains that await me,

through love of You. Therefore I say with St. Francis, "May I die, O Lord! through love of You, Who, through love of me, did not disdain to die."

GLORY BE TO THE FATHER   Glory be to the Father, and to the Son, and to the Holy Spirit, as it was in the beginning, is now and ever shall be, world without end. Amen.

THE FATIMA PRAYER   O my Jesus, forgive us our sins, save us from the fires of hell, lead all souls to heaven, especially those in most need of Thy mercy.

CONCLUDING PRAYERS   *Upon completing the recitation of the Holy Rosary, the following prayers are customary, but others too may be added according to one's devotion and preference.*

HAIL HOLY QUEEN   Hail Holy Queen, Mother of Mercy, hail our life, our sweetness and our hope. To thee do we cry, poor banished children of Eve, to thee do we send up our sighs, mourning and weeping in this vale of tears. Turn then, most gracious advocate, thine eyes of mercy towards us, and after this, our exile, show unto us the blessed fruit of thy womb, Jesus. O clement, O loving, O sweet Virgin Mary. Pray for us O holy Mother of God, that we may be made worthy of the promises of Christ.

Let Us Pray   O God, Whose only begotten son, by His life, death and resurrection, has purchased for us the rewards of eternal life, grant we beseech You, that meditating on these mysteries of the most Holy Rosary of the Blessed Virgin

Mary, we may both imitate what they contain and obtain what they promise, through the same Christ our Lord. Amen.

PRAYER TO SAINT MICHAEL THE ARCHANGEL   Holy Michael, the Archangel, defend us in the day of battle. Be our safeguard against the wickedness and snares of the devil. May God rebuke him, we humbly pray; and do thou, O Prince of the heavenly hosts, by the power of God thrust down into hell Satan and all the evil spirits who wander through the world seeking the ruin of souls. Amen.

MEMORARE   Remember, O most gracious Virgin Mary, that never was it known that anyone who fled to thy protection, implored thy help, or sought thine intercession was left unaided. Inspired by this confidence, I fly unto thee, O Virgin of virgins, my mother; to thee do I come, before you I stand, sinful and sorrowful. O Mother of the Word Incarnate, despise not my petitions, but in thy mercy hear and answer me. Amen.

May the Divine Assistance remain always with us, and may the souls of the faithful departed, through the mercy of God rest in peace. Amen.

The Glorious Mysteries

The Resurrection

THE FRUIT OF THIS MYSTERY

Sharing in Our Lady's Joy at the resurrection of her son

E CONTEMPLATE HOW, THE third day after His death, Jesus Christ rose again triumphant and glorious, to die no more. Let us consider the glory of our Redeemer when He arose from the sepulchre, after having vanquished Satan, and delivered the human race from bondage. How great is the folly of the sinner who, having been once delivered from the tyranny of the devil, consents to become again his slave for some wretched gain or some miserable pleasure of this world! Let us pray to the Blessed Virgin to unite us by love so closely to Jesus Christ that we may never again by mortal sin become the slaves of Lucifer.

OUR FATHER   Our Father, Who art in Heaven, hallowed be Thy name, Thy kingdom come, Thy will be done, on earth as it is in heaven. Give us this day our daily bread; and forgive us our trespasses, as we forgive those who trespass against us; and lead us not into temptation, but deliver us from evil. Amen.

HAIL MARY (10)   Hail Mary, Full of Grace, the Lord is with thee. Blessed art thou among women and blessed is the fruit of thy womb, Jesus. Holy Mary, Mother of God, pray for us sinners now, and at the hour of our death. Amen.

1. With reverential force they took Jesus from Our Lady's arms, and having embalmed Him, wrapped Him in a linen cloth already prepared, upon which our Lord wished to leave to the world His image impressed, as may be seen at the present day in Turin. And now they bear Him to the sepulchre. The sorrowful funeral train sets forth; the disciples place Him on their shoulders; hosts of angels from heaven accompany Him; the holy women follow Him; and the afflicted mother likewise, as they journey to the tomb. When they had reached the appointed place, how gladly would Mary have buried herself there alive with her son! The Virgin earnestly desired that her soul should be buried with the body of Christ. And Mary herself made this revelation

to St. Bridget, "I can truly say, that at the burial of my son, one sepulchre contained as it were two hearts."

2. They take the stone and close up in the holy sepulchre the body of Jesus, that great treasure, greater than any in heaven and on earth. And here let us remark, that Mary left her heart buried with Jesus, because Jesus was all her treasure. And where shall we keep our hearts buried? With creatures? In the mire? And why not with Jesus, Who, although He has ascended to heaven, has wished to remain, not dead but alive, in the most holy sacrament of the altar, precisely in order that He might have our company and possess our hearts?

3. Many Christians submit to great fatigue, and expose themselves to many dangers, to visit the places in the Holy Land where our most loving Saviour was born, suffered, and died. We need not undertake so long a journey, or expose ourselves to so many dangers; the same Lord is near us, and dwells in the church, only a few steps distant from our houses. If pilgrims consider it a great thing to bring back a little dust from the crib, or from the holy sepulchre in which Jesus was buried, with what ardour should not we visit the Most Blessed Sacrament, where the same Jesus is in person, and where we can go without encountering so much fatigue and so many dangers! O holy mystery! O sacred Host! Where is it that God manifests His power the most, if it is not in this Host? For this Host contains all that God has ever done for us. Let us not envy the blessed who are in heaven, since on earth we have the same Lord, with greater wonders of His love.

4. It is said that at the death of Christ many saints then arose, and, leaving the graves, appeared to many. These were the just, who had believed and hoped in Jesus Christ; and God desired thus to honour them, as a reward for their faith and confidence in the future Messiah. Moreover, the centurion, and the other soldiers who were under him, who had put the Saviour to death, were themselves moved with the miracles of the darkness and earthquake, and recognised Him as the Son of God. These soldiers were the first-fruits of the Gentiles, who embraced the faith of Jesus Christ after they had put Him to death. Through His merits, they had grace to understand their sin and to hope for pardon.

5. Before leaving the sepulchre, Our Lady blessed the sacred stone, saying, "Oh happy stone, that now encloses that body which was contained nine months in my womb, I bless you, and envy you; I leave you to guard my son for me, Who is my only good, my only love." And then turning to the Eternal Father, she said, "Oh Father, to You I recommend Him, who is Your son and mine." Thus bidding a last fare-well to her son, and to the sepulchre, she returned to her own house. This poor mother went away so afflicted and sad, according to St. Bernard, that she moved many to tears even against their will.

6. The two sisters of our Lady wrapped her in a veil as a widow, covering as it were her whole countenance. Then, passing, on her return, before the cross, still wet with the blood of her Jesus, Our Lady was the first to adore it, "Oh holy cross, she exclaimed, I kiss you and adore you; for You are no longer an infamous wood, but a throne of love, and

an altar of mercy, consecrated by the blood of the divine Lamb, who has been sacrificed upon you, for the salvation of the world." She then left the cross and returned to her house; there the afflicted mother casts her eyes around, and no longer sees her Jesus; but instead of the presence of her dear son, all the memorials of His holy life and cruel death are before her. There she is reminded of the embraces she gave her son in the stable of Bethlehem, of the conversations held with Him for so many years in the shop of Nazareth: she is reminded of their mutual affection, of His loving looks, of the words of eternal life that came forth from that divine mouth. The sorrowful mother turned to St. John, and said mournfully, "Ah, John, where is your master?" Then she asked of Magdalen, "Daughter, tell me where is your beloved?" Mary weeps, and all those who are with her weep. Let me, oh my Lady, let me weep; You are innocent, I am guilty. Entreat her to permit you to weep with her, but not for long, for the Lord rose gloriously on the third day.

7. Let us rejoice at seeing in His risen glory our Saviour, our Father, the best Friend we possess. Let us rejoice, too, for our own sakes, because the Resurrection of Jesus Christ is for us a sure pledge of our own resurrection and of the glory we hope one day to have in Heaven in our soul and body. The hope of the resurrection gave courage to the Martyrs to suffer with gladness all the evils of life, and the most cruel torments of tyrants. None will rejoice with Jesus Christ save those who are willing to suffer in this world with Him; nor will he obtain the crown who does not fight as he ought to fight. Let us labour the more to continue in the grace of God, and continually pray for perseverance in God's friendship.

8. We find that after His resurrection Jesus Christ entered, though the doors were closed, into the house in which the apostles were assembled, and stood in the midst of them. The mystic meaning of this miracle is that the Lord does not enter into our souls unless we keep the door of the senses shut. If, then, we wish Jesus Christ to dwell within us, we must keep the doors of our senses closed against dangerous occasions, otherwise the devil will make us his slaves.

9. The delights of the soul infinitely surpass all the pleasures of the senses. Even in this life, Divine love infuses such sweetness into the soul when God communicates Himself to it that the body is raised from the earth. St. Peter of Alcantara once fell into such an ecstasy of love that, taking hold of a tree, he drew it up from the roots, and raised it with him on high. So great is the sweetness of Divine love, that the holy Martyrs, in the midst of their torments, felt no pain, but were on the contrary filled with joy. Hence when St. Laurence was laid on a red-hot gridiron, the fervour of Divine love made him insensible to the burning heat of the fire. Even on sinners who weep for their sins, God bestows consolations which exceed all earthly pleasures. Hence St. Bernard says, "If it be so sweet to weep for You, what must it be to rejoice in You!"

10. "Your sorrow", says the Saviour to encourage us, "shall be turned into joy." So great are the delights of Paradise that they can neither be explained nor understood by us mortals. Beauties like to the beauties of Paradise, eye has never seen; harmonies like unto the harmonies of Paradise, ear has never heard; nor has ever human heart gained the

comprehension of the joys God has prepared for those that love Him. Beautiful is the sight of a landscape adorned with hills, plains, woods, and views of the sea. Beautiful is the sight of a garden abounding with fruits, flowers, and fountains. Oh, how much more beautiful is Paradise! To understand how great the joys of Paradise are, it is enough to know that in that blessed realm resides a God omnipotent, Whose care it is to render happy His beloved souls. There You shall not find any thing displeasing to thyself, and every thing You desire You shall find. In Paradise there is no night; no seasons of winter and summer; but one perpetual day of unvaried serenity, and one perpetual spring of unvaried delight. No more persecutions or jealousies are there; for there all sincerely love one another, and each rejoices in each other's good as if it were his own. No more bodily infirmities or pains are there, for the body is no longer subject to suffering; no poverty is there, for every one is rich to the full, not having anything more to desire; no more fears are there, for the soul being confirmed in grace can sin no more, nor lose that supreme good which it possesses.

GLORY BE TO THE FATHER   Glory be to the Father, and to the Son, and to the Holy Spirit, as it was in the beginning, is now and ever shall be, world without end. Amen.

THE FATIMA PRAYER   O my Jesus, forgive us our sins, save us from the fires of hell, lead all souls to heaven, especially those in most need of Thy mercy.

The Ascension

THE FRUIT OF THIS MYSTERY

That our hearts may follow the Lord Jesus into heaven

N THE ASCENSION OF our Blessed Lord we contemplate how, forty days after His Resurrection,
He ascended into Heaven in triumph, surrounded
by great glory, in the sight of His holy Mother and His
disciples. "Lift up your gates, O you princes, and be you
lifted up, O eternal gates; and the King of glory shall enter

in." O Paradise! O Paradise! When, O Lord, shall I see You face to face, and embrace You?

OUR FATHER   Our Father, Who art in Heaven, hallowed be Thy name, Thy kingdom come, Thy will be done, on earth as it is in heaven. Give us this day our daily bread; and forgive us our trespasses, as we forgive those who trespass against us; and lead us not into temptation, but deliver us from evil. Amen.

HAIL MARY (10)   Hail Mary, Full of Grace, the Lord is with thee. Blessed art thou among women and blessed is the fruit of thy womb, Jesus. Holy Mary, Mother of God, pray for us sinners now, and at the hour of our death. Amen.

1. The rightful home of the risen Saviour was Heaven, the home of the Blessed, but Jesus wished to remain still on earth for forty days, appearing again and again to His disciples before He ascended into Heaven, in order to strengthen their Faith in His Resurrection and to give them consolation and hope. Meanwhile the Angels ardently desired to have their King in their heavenly country, and hence they were continually supplicating Him, "Come, O Lord, come quickly, now that You have redeemed men, come to Your kingdom and dwell with us."

2. Behold now the solemn hour has arrived and our Blessed Saviour ascends Mount Olivet with His Apostles and disciples to about the number of one hundred and twenty. Then, raising His hands to Heaven, Jesus blesses them and ascends into the skies in triumph, surrounded by great glory. When

a monarch makes His solemn entry into His kingdom, He does not pass through the gates of His capital city, for they are removed to make way for Him on the occasion. Hence, when Jesus Christ now enters Paradise, the Angels cry out, "Lift up your gates, O princes, and be lifted up, O eternal gates, that the King of Glory may enter in."

3. Hope is a supernatural virtue by which we confidently expect, in virtue of God's promise, the endless happiness of Heaven and the means necessary for its attainment. The first and foremost object of our hope, the object by excellence, is the possession of God in Heaven. The hope of eternal happiness is inseparably united with love, for only in Heaven will the completion and perfection of love be found. As long, therefore, as our soul is not perfectly united with God in Heaven, it will never enjoy true peace. As long as the soul is separated from her last end she shall continue to sigh with the prophet, "Behold in peace is my bitterness most bitter." Yes, my God, I live in peace in this valley of tears, for such is Your holy will; but I cannot but remember, with unspeakable pain, that I am not as yet perfectly united with You, the Source of all peace and rest, the goal of my heart's desire.

4. Before Jesus Christ died for us, Paradise was closed against us; in His Ascension we see that Jesus has opened it for all those that love Him. Ah, what a pity that, after our Saviour has suffered so much to obtain Paradise, this happy kingdom, so many foolish sinners should renounce it and give themselves up to hell for worthless pleasures, for a mere nothing! Let us beseech Mary to obtain for us the light to

see clearly how miserable are the goods of this world, and how great the delights that God offers in the world to come to those that love Him.

5. The Lord mounts the skies leading a glorious number of captives. All the multitude of blessed souls who have come forth from Limbo ascend to Heaven with Him. Our Saviour has opened Paradise for all who love Him. O my Jesus, when I look upon my sins I am ashamed to seek for Paradise, but when I look on You upon the Cross I cannot cease to hope for Heaven. Ah, my Jesus, when will the day arrive that shall free me from all danger of losing You?

6. After the ascension of Jesus Christ, Mary remained on earth to attend to the propagation of the faith. Hence the disciples of Jesus had recourse to her, and she resolved their doubts, comforted them in their persecutions, and encouraged them to labour for the divine glory and for the salvation of the souls redeemed by her son. She, indeed, willingly remained on earth, understanding this to be the will of God for the good of the Church; but she could not but feel the pain of being far from the presence and sight of her beloved son, Who had ascended into heaven. "Where your treasure is," said the Redeemer, "there will your heart be also."

7. There is no doubt that attachment to the goods of earth renders the death of the worldly bitter and miserable, as the Holy Spirit says, "Oh! death, how bitter is the remembrance of you to a man that has peace in his possessions!" But because the saints die detached from the things of

the world, their death is not bitter, but sweet, lovely, and precious. "Blessed are the dead who die in the Lord", this is how Scripture describes those happy souls that pass into eternity. They are already detached, and, as it were, dead to all affections for terrestrial things, having found in God alone there every good.

8. The Almighty complains that many souls go about seeking for fleeting and miserable pleasures from creatures, and leave Him, Who is the infinite good and fountain of all joy. Wherefore God, Who loves us, and desires to see us happy, cries out and makes known to all, "If any thirst, let them come to Me." The key which opens the channels of this blessed water is holy prayer, which obtains every good for us in virtue of the Lord's promise, "Ask and you shall receive." God desires to give us His graces; but He will have us pray for them. O my Jesus, with the Samaritan woman, I beseech You, give me this water of Your love, which may make me forget the earth, to live only for You, O amiable, infinite one. My soul is a barren soil, which produces nothing but the weeds and thorns of sin; oh, water it with Your grace, so that it may bring forth some fruits to Your glory, before death takes me out of this world. O fountain of living water, O sovereign good, how many times have I left You for the puddles of this earth, which have deprived me of Your love! Oh, would that I had died before I offended You! But for the future I will seek after nothing but You, O my God.

9. Should a Christian after the Ascension of the Redeemer into heaven, say to Him, Lord, if You wish to show us Your affection, remain with us on our altars under the appearance

of bread, that we may be able to find You whenever we wish, would not such a demand be regarded as the extreme of temerity? But, what no man could ever even imagine, our Saviour has invented and accomplished. But, alas! Where is our gratitude for so great a favour? If a prince came from a distance to a village for the purpose of being visited by a peasant, how great would be the ingratitude of the peasant if he refused to visit his sovereign or if he paid him only a passing visit?

10. In the life the princes of the earth and the worldly rich are deemed fortunate, but the saints, who live in poverty and humiliations, are despised. O faithful souls who love God, be not troubled at seeing yourselves in contempt and tribulations on this earth, "Your sorrow shall be turned into joy." On the day of judgement you will be called truly fortunate, and will have the honour of being declared as belonging to the court of Jesus Christ. Oh! How beautiful will then be the appearance of St Peter of Alcantara, who was despised as an apostate! of St John of God, who was treated as a fool! of St Peter Celestine, who, after having renounced the papal throne, died in prison! Oh! How great will then be the honours of so many martyrs who have been torn to pieces by their executioners! But on the other hand, how horrible will be the appearance of Herod, of Pilate, of Nero, and so many other great men of this earth, who are now damned! O lovers of the world, in the valley, in the valley I expect you. There, without doubt you will change your sentiments, there you will weep over your folly. Miserable beings, who for the sake of making a figure for a short time on the theatre of this world, will afterward have

to act the part of reprobate in the tragedy of judgement. The elect will then be placed on the right; according to the apostle, they will, for their greater glory, be raised in the air above the clouds, and will go with the angels to meet Jesus Christ descending from heaven. We shall be taken up together with them to meet Christ into the air. But the damned, like so many goats destined for the slaughter, will be compelled to remain at the left, waiting for the Judge, Who will publicly pronounce sentence of condemnation against all His enemies.

GLORY BE TO THE FATHER   Glory be to the Father, and to the Son, and to the Holy Spirit, as it was in the beginning, is now and ever shall be, world without end. Amen.

THE FATIMA PRAYER   O my Jesus, forgive us our sins, save us from the fires of hell, lead all souls to heaven, especially those in most need of Thy mercy.

The Descent of the Holy Spirit

THE FRUIT OF THIS MYSTERY

A desire to share the one true faith with others

HE ETERNAL FATHER WAS not content with giving us His son, Jesus Christ, to save us by His death, He has given us also the Holy Spirit to dwell always in our souls and keep them inflamed with His holy love. Hence, when the Holy Spirit descended upon the Apostles, He appeared in the form of tongues of fire. This is the holy fire that inflamed the saints with the desire to do great things for God, that enabled them to love their most cruel enemies, to seek after contempt, to renounce all the riches and honours of the world, and even to embrace torments and death.

OUR FATHER   Our Father, Who art in Heaven, hallowed be Thy name, Thy kingdom come, Thy will be done, on earth as it is in heaven. Give us this day our daily bread; and forgive us our trespasses, as we forgive those who trespass against us; and lead us not into temptation, but deliver us from evil. Amen.

HAIL MARY (10)   Hail Mary, Full of Grace, the Lord is with thee. Blessed art thou among women and blessed is the fruit of thy womb, Jesus. Holy Mary, Mother of God, pray for us sinners now, and at the hour of our death. Amen.

1. The Holy Spirit is that divine bond which unites the Father with the Son; it is He Who unites our souls, through love, with God. The chains of the world are chains of death, but the bonds of the Holy Spirit are bonds of Eternal life, because they bind us to God, Who is our true and only Life. Let us also remember that all the lights, inspirations, divine calls, all the good acts we have performed during our life, all our acts of contrition, of confidence in the divine mercy, of love, of resignation, have been the gifts of the Holy Spirit.

2. "The Spirit also helps our infirmity; for we know not what we should pray for as we ought; but the Spirit Himself asks for us with unspeakable groanings." Thus, it, is the Holy Spirit Who prays for us; for we know not what to ask,

but the Holy Spirit teaches us what we should pray for. O Holy and Divine Spirit, come into my heart and teach me to pray as I ought. Give me strength not to neglect prayer in times of weariness and dryness. I have been lost by my sins. You desire my sanctification and salvation, and I, too, earnestly desire to become holy. I love You, my sovereign Good, my Love, my All, and because I love You, I give myself wholly to You.

3. The nine days of prayer to the Holy Spirit was the first Novena ever celebrated. It was participated in by the holy Apostles and the most holy Mary in the supper-room and it resulted in so many remarkable wonders and gifts; principally by the gift of the same Holy Spirit, a gift merited for us by the Passion of Jesus Christ Himself. Endeavour, by devout exercises, and especially by prayer, to be made partakers of this same Gift, since God has promised it to all who asks for it with humility, "Your Father from heaven will give the good Spirit to them that ask Him."

4. God had ordered, in the ancient law, that there should be a fire kept continually burning on His altar. The altars of God are our hearts, where He desires that the fire of His divine love should always be burning; and therefore the Eternal Father, not satisfied with having given us His son Jesus Christ, to save us by His death, would also give us the Holy Spirit, that He might dwell in our souls, and keep them constantly on fire with love. And Jesus Himself declared, that He had come into the world on purpose to inflame our hearts with this holy fire, and that He desired nothing more than to see it kindled. Forgetting, therefore, the injuries and

ingratitude He received from men on this earth, when He had ascended into heaven He sent down upon us the Holy Spirit. Hence it was that the Holy Spirit chose to appear in the supper-room under the form of tongues of fire. This was the holy fire which has inflamed the saints to do so great things for God, to love their enemies, to desire contempt, to deprive themselves of all earthly goods, and to embrace with delight even torments and death.

5. O Holy and Divine Spirit, I believe that You are really God, but one only God with the Father and the Son. I adore You, and acknowledge You as the giver of all those lights by which You have made known to me the evil which I have committed in offending You, and the obligation which I am under of loving You. I thank You for them, and I repent with my whole heart of having offended You. I have deserved that You should abandon me in my darkness; but I see that You have not yet forsaken me. Continue, O Eternal Spirit, to enlighten me, and to make me know more and more Your infinite goodness; and give me strength to love You for the future with my whole heart.

6. Love fertilises the good desires, the holy purposes and the good works of our souls: these are the flowers and fruits which the grace of the Holy Spirit produces. Love is also called dew, because it cools the heat of bad passions and of temptations. Therefore the Holy Spirit is also called refreshment and cooling in the heat. This dew descends into our hearts in the time of prayer. A quarter of an hour's prayer is sufficient to appease every passion of hatred or of inordinate love, however ardent it may be. Holy meditation

is this cellar where love is set in order, so that we love our neighbour as ourselves, and God above everything. He who loves God loves prayer; and he that loves not prayer will find it morally impossible to overcome his passions.

7. The Holy Spirit is called "sweet guest of the soul", for the Holy Spirit never forsakes a soul if He is not driven away from it. God, then, dwells in a soul that loves Him; but He declares that He is not satisfied if we do not love Him with our whole heart. He will have no rivals in the heart that loves Him; and when He sees that He is not the only object loved, He is jealous of those creatures who divide with Him the heart which He desires to have all to Himself. Because He does not want the world to take even a part of that love which He desires to have all to Himself, He praises His spouse by calling her "a garden enclosed", a garden closed against all earthly love.

8. We contemplate how Jesus Christ, seated at the right hand of His Father, sent down the Holy Spirit to the chamber where the apostles with the Virgin Mary were assembled. Before receiving the Holy Spirit, the apostles were so feeble, so cold, in the love of God, that, at the time of the Passion of our Lord, one betrayed Him, another denied Him, and all abandoned Him; but as soon as they had all received the Holy Spirit, they were so much inflamed with love that they gave up their lives generously for Jesus Christ. "He who loves, does not labour." He who loves God feels no affliction under crosses, but rather rejoices, let us ask of Mary to obtain for us from the Holy Spirit the gift of divine love; for then all the crosses of this life will seem sweet to us.

9. The humble retire and choose the lowest place, hence, the Blessed Virgin, when she was in the "upper room" with the apostles, she wished to take the lowest place. Before the Day of Pentecost we are told that "All the apostles were persevering with one mind in prayer, with the woman and Mary the mother of Jesus." St. Luke was well antiquated with the merit of the divine mother, and on account of which he would have wanted to give her the first place; but because she always chose to take the lowest place, the saint was compelled to describe her thus: Justly has the last become first, who, when she was first of all, was recorded as last.

10. Holy Spirit, Divine Paraclete, I adore You with the most profound submission, and I repeat a thousand times with the seraphs who are before Your throne: Holy, Holy, Holy! I offer You my heart cold as it is, and I supplicate You to let a ray of Your light and a spark of Your fire enter therein to melt the hardened ice of my iniquities. You Who have filled with immense graces the soul of Mary, and inflamed with a holy zeal the hearts of the apostles, vouchsafe also to set on fire my heart with Your love. You are a Divine Spirit; fortify me against evil spirits: You are a fire; enkindle in me the fire of Your love: You are a light; enlighten me so that I may know eternal things: You are a dove; give me great purity of heart: You are a breath that is full of sweetness; dissipate the storms that my passions raise up against me: You are a tongue; teach me the manner of praising You without ceasing. You are a cloud; cover me with the shadow of Your protection: and if, finally, You are the author of all heavenly gifts, ah, I beseech You to grant them to me: vivify me by Your grace, sanctify me by Your charity, govern me by

Your wisdom, adopt me by Your bounty as Your child, and save me by Your infinite mercy, so that I may never cease to bless You, to praise You, to love You, at first during my life on this earth, and afterwards for all eternity in heaven.

GLORY BE TO THE FATHER   Glory be to the Father, and to the Son, and to the Holy Spirit, as it was in the beginning, is now and ever shall be, world without end. Amen.

THE FATIMA PRAYER   O my Jesus, forgive us our sins, save us from the fires of hell, lead all souls to heaven, especially those in most need of Thy mercy.

The Assumption of the Blessed Virgin

THE FRUIT OF THIS MYSTERY

The grace of a holy death

I N THE ASSUMPTION OF Our Blessed Lady, we contemplate how Mary, twelve years after the resurrection of Jesus Christ, departed this life, and was carried up by angels to heaven. The death of Mary was full of peace and consolation, because her life had been all holy. Our death will not be like hers, for our sins will then be a subject of alarm. But hear this my friends, for anyone who renounces a bad life and consecrates himself to the service of Mary, this good Mother will not fail to comfort him in that last moment, and obtain for him the grace of dying consoled, as she has done to so many of her faithful servants. Let us place ourselves, then, under her protection, with the firm purpose to amend our lives; and let us always ask her to assist us in the hour of death.

OUR FATHER   Our Father, Who art in Heaven, hallowed be Thy name, Thy kingdom come, Thy will be done, on earth as it is in heaven. Give us this day our daily bread; and forgive us our trespasses, as we forgive those who trespass against us; and lead us not into temptation, but deliver us from evil. Amen.

HAIL MARY (10)   Hail Mary, Full of Grace, the Lord is with thee. Blessed art thou among women and blessed is the fruit of thy womb, Jesus. Holy Mary, Mother of God, pray for us sinners now, and at the hour of our death. Amen.

1. Death being the punishment of sin, it would seem that the divine mother, all holy and exempt from every stain, should not be subject to death, nor suffer the same misfortune as the children of Adam, who are infected by the poison of sin. But God, wishing Mary in all things to be like to Jesus, required, as the Son had died, that the mother should also die; and because He wishes to give to the just an example of the blessed death prepared for them, He decreed that the Virgin should die, but by a sweet and happy death.

2. It was said of Mary in the sacred canticles, "Who is she that goes up by the desert as a pillar of smoke of aromatic spices, of myrrh, and frankincense, and of all the powders of the perfumer?" Her entire mortification was prefigured in the myrrh, her fervent prayers were signified by the incense, and all her holy virtues united to her perfect charity towards God, kindled in her a flame so great, that her holy soul, wholly devoted to, and consumed by divine love, arose continually to God as a pillar of smoke that on all sides breathed a sweet odour. As the loving Virgin lived, so she died. As the divine love gave her life, so it gave her death; for she died as the holy Doctors and Fathers of the Church generally affirm, of no other infirmity than pure love.

3. St. John saw Mary represented in that woman clothed with the sun, who held the moon under her feet. Interpreters explain the moon to signify the goods of this earth, that are uncertain, and change as the moon does. All these goods Mary never had in her heart, but always despised them and kept them under her feet; living in this world as a solitary turtle-dove in a desert; placing her affection on no earthly thing, so that it was said of her, "The voice of the turtle-dove is heard in our land."

4. If Mary then loved no other good than Jesus, He being in heaven, in heaven were all her desires. The cell of Mary was heaven, for being in heaven, with her affection, she made it her continual abode. Her school was eternity for she was always detached from temporal possessions. Her teacher, divine truth: for she was always guided in her actions by the divine light. Her mirror, the Divinity; for she looked upon

nothing but God, in order to conform always to the divine will. Her ornament, devotion: for she was always ready to fulfil the divine commands. Her repose, union with God: for her peace was only in uniting herself with God. In a word, the place and treasure of her heart was God alone.

5. The most holy Virgin consoled her loving heart during this cruel separation, by visiting the holy places of Palestine, where her son had been in His lifetime: she often visited now the stable of Bethlehem, where her son was born; now the workshop at Nazareth, where her son had lived so many years poor and despised; now the garden of Gethsemane, where her son commenced His passion: now the hall of Pilate, where He was scourged; the place where He was crowned; but more often she visited Calvary, where her son had expired; and the holy sepulchre, where she finally had left Him. And thus the most loving mother used to soothe the pains of her cruel exile. But this was not enough to satisfy her heart, which could not find its perfect rest upon this earth; hence her continual sighs were ascending to her Lord, as she exclaimed with David, but with more ardent love, "Who will give me wings like a dove to fly to my God and there to find my rest? As the wounded stag pants for the fountain, so my soul, wounded by Your love, oh my God, desires and sighs for You." Wherefore not being willing to defer any longer consolation to His beloved, behold, He graciously hears her desire and calls her to His kingdom.

6. The Lord, some days before Our Lady's death, sent to her the angel Gabriel, the same who once announced to her that she was the blessed woman chosen to be the mother of

God, "My Lady and Queen", said the angel to her, "God has already graciously heard your holy desires, and He has sent me to tell you to prepare to leave the earth, for He wishes you with Him in paradise. Come then, to take possession of your kingdom, for I and all its holy citizens await and desire you." At this happy annunciation what should our most humble and holy Virgin do but conceal herself more deeply in the centre of her most profound humility, and reply in those same words with which she answered St. Gabriel when he announced to her that she was to become Mother of God, "Behold the handmaid of the Lord. He in His pure goodness has chosen me and made me His mother; now He calls me to paradise. I neither merited the one or the other honour; but since He wishes to manifest His infinite liberality towards me, I am ready to go where He wishes. Behold the handmaid of the Lord, may the will of my Lord always be fulfilled in me."

7. After receiving this precious intelligence, she imparted it to St. John, and we may imagine with what grief and tender emotion he heard this news; he who for so many years had been near her as a son, and had enjoyed the celestial conversation of this most holy mother. She then visited anew the holy places of Jerusalem, tenderly taking leave of them, especially of Calvary, where her beloved son had died. And then she returned to her poor dwelling to prepare for death. During this time the angels did not cease to come and visit this their beloved queen, consoling themselves with the thought that they should soon see her crowned in heaven. Many authors assert, that before she died, by a divine miracle, the apostles and also some of the disciples

came from the different places where they were dispersed, and all assembled in the apartment of Mary, and that when she saw all these her dear children united together in her presence, she thus addressed them, "My dear children, for love of you, and to help you, my son left me on this earth. But now the holy faith is spread throughout the world, already the fruit of the divine seed is grown up; hence my divine son, seeing that my assistance was no longer needed upon the earth, and compassionating me for the pain of separation, has graciously heard my desire to depart from this life, and go to see Him in glory. If I leave you, my heart does not leave you; I will carry with me the great love I bear you, and it shall always remain with me."

8. At these sad tidings, who can realise how great were the tears and lamentations of these holy disciples, knowing that they were shortly to be separated from their mother? Then, they all in tears exclaimed, "Oh Mary, are you to leave us? It is true that this earth is not a worthy and fit place for you, and that we are not worthy to enjoy the society of the Mother of God; but remember that you are our mother; You have until now enlightened us in our doubts, consoled our sorrows, strengthened us in persecutions, and how can you now abandon us, leaving us alone without your comfort in the midst of so many enemies and so many conflicts? We have already lost on earth Jesus, our master and our Father, Who has ascended into heaven; we have since been consoled by you, our mother; and now how can you leave us orphans, without father or mother? Oh remain with us, oh our Lady! or take us with you." But Our Lady responds sweetly, "No, my children, this is not according to the will

of God; content yourselves to do what lie has appointed for you and for me. To you it yet remains to labour on the earth for the glory of your Redeemer, and to perfect your eternal crown. I do not leave you to abandon you, but to help you more by my intercession with God in heaven."

9. Then she begged them to give burial to her body after death, blessed them, and directed St. John that after her death he should give her two garments to two virgins who had served her for some time, and then she decently composed herself upon her poor little bed, where she laid herself to await death, and with death the meeting with her divine spouse, who shortly was to come and take her with Him to the kingdom of the blessed. Behold, she already feels in her heart a great joy, the forerunner of the coming of the spouse, which overwhelms her with a great and new sweetness. The holy apostles, seeing that Mary already was about to depart from this earth, burst forth into fresh weeping, and knelt around her bed: some kissed her holy feet, others asked her special blessing, one recommended to her some particular necessity of his, and all wept bitterly, for their hearts were pierced with grief at being obliged to separate forever in this life from their beloved Lady. And she, their most loving mother, compassionated all, consoled all, promising to some her protection, blessing others with peculiar affection, and encouraging others to labour for the conversion of the world; especially did she call St. Peter to her, and as head of the Church, and vicar of her son, she recommended to him in particular the propagation of the faith, promising him her special protection from heaven. But in a very special manner did she call to her St. John, who felt a greater

sorrow than all the others at the moment of separation from that holy mother; and the most grateful Lady, calling to mind the affection and attention with which this holy disciple had served her through all the years they had passed on earth since the death of her son, said to him with great tenderness, "My John, I thank you for all the assistance you have afforded me; my son, be certain that I never will be ungrateful to you for it. If I leave you now, I am going to pray for you. Remain in peace in this life until we meet in heaven, where I will await You. Do not forget me; in all your necessities call me to your aid, for I never will forget you, my beloved son. My son, I bless You, I leave you my benediction; farewell, until we meet again."

10. But the death of Mary draws near. The divine love, with its blessed and ardent flames, have almost entirely consumed the vital spirits, the celestial phoenix is going to lose her life in the midst of this fire. Then the host of angels come to meet her, as if to be ready for the great triumph with which they are to accompany her to paradise. Mary was indeed consoled at the sight of these holy spirits; but not fully consoled, for she did not yet see her beloved Jesus, Who was the whole love of her heart. Hence she often repeated to the angels who descended to salute her, "I adjure you, oh daughters of Jerusalem, if you find my beloved, that you tell Him that I languish with love. Oh holy angels! Oh blessed citizens of the heavenly Jerusalem! You come kindly to console me, and you all console me with your sweet presence; I thank you, but you all do not fully satisfy me, for I do not yet see my son coming to console me, go, if you love me, return to paradise, and tell my beloved, from me, that I languish

and faint for His love. Tell Him to come, and come quickly, for I am dying with my desire to see Him." But behold, Jesus Himself comes to take His mother to the kingdom of the blessed. The son appeared to Mary before she expired, with the cross in His hand, to show the special glory He had obtained from the redemption, having by His death made the acquisition of this great creature, who through the ages of eternity was to honour Him more than all men and all angels. He gave to her the holy viaticum, saying to her, tenderly, "Take, oh my mother, from My hands, that same body which you have given Me." And the mother having received with the greatest love that final communion, with her last sighs said to Him, "My son, into Your hands I commend my spirit; I recommend to You this soul that You, in Your goodness did create even from the beginning, rich in so many graces, and by a peculiar privilege have preserved from every stain of sin. I commend to You my body, from which You have deigned to take flesh and blood. I commend to You, also, these my dear children, they are afflicted at my departure; give them strength to do great things for Your glory."

GLORY BE TO THE FATHER   Glory be to the Father, and to the Son, and to the Holy Spirit, as it was in the beginning, is now and ever shall be, world without end. Amen.

THE FATIMA PRAYER   O my Jesus, forgive us our sins, save us from the fires of hell, lead all souls to heaven, especially those in most need of Thy mercy.

The Coronation of the Blessed Virgin Mary and the Glory of all the Angels and Saints

THE FRUIT OF THIS MYSTERY

Sharing in the joy of Our Lady in her glory

N THE CORONATION OF Our Blessed Lady we consider how Mary was crowned by her Divine Son, and we contemplate at the same time the glory of all the saints. When Mary was crowned in heaven by the hand of God, she was also appointed to be our advocate; for this reason, Blessed Amadeus says that she prays for us incessantly. It is true that Mary prays for all men, but she especially prays for those that often and confidently have recourse to her intercession. Let us beseech her always to pray for us, by saying with the Church, "Holy Mary, Mother of God, pray for us".

OUR FATHER   Our Father, Who art in Heaven, hallowed be Thy name, Thy kingdom come, Thy will be done, on earth as it is in heaven. Give us this day our daily bread; and forgive us our trespasses, as we forgive those who trespass against us; and lead us not into temptation, but deliver us from evil. Amen.

HAIL MARY (10)   Hail Mary, Full of Grace, the Lord is with thee. Blessed art thou among women and blessed is the fruit of thy womb, Jesus. Holy Mary, Mother of God, pray for us sinners now, and at the hour of our death. Amen.

1. The end of the life of Mary having now arrived, there was heard, in the apartment where she lay, a great harmony; and also, as it was revealed to St. Bridget, a great brightness was seen. By this harmony and unusual splendour the holy Apostles perceived that Mary was then departing, at which they broke forth again in tears and prayers, and raising their hands, with one voice exclaimed, "Oh, our mother, now you are going to heaven, and are leaving us, give us your last benediction, and do not forget us in our misery." And Mary, turning her eyes around upon them all, as if bidding

them for the last time farewell, said, "Farewell, my children: I bless you; do not fear that I shall forget you." And now death came, not indeed clothed in mourning and sadness, as it comes to others, but adorned with light and joy. Divine love came to cut the thread of that noble life. And as a lamp before going out, her life, amid these last flickerings, flashed forth more brightly, and then expired. Thus, this beautiful soul, wrapped in the flame of her charity, and in the midst of her amorous sighs, breathed forth a greater sigh of love, expired and died; and thus that great soul, that beautiful dove of our Lord, was released from the bonds of this life, and entered into the glory of the blessed, where she sits, and will sit, as queen of paradise, for all eternity. Now Mary has left the earth, now she is in heaven. From thence this kind mother looks down upon us, who are still in this valley of tears. She compassionates us and promises us her support if we wish for it. Let us ask her always that by the merits of her blessed death she may obtain for us a happy death; and if it please God, that she may obtain for us to die on a Saturday, which is dedicated to her honour, or on one of her feast days, as she has obtained for so many of her servants.

2. If we love this our mother, we ought to congratulate ourselves more upon her glory than upon our own particular consolation. What son does not rejoice, although separated from his mother, if he knows that she is going to take possession of a kingdom? Mary is to be crowned queen of heaven, and shall we not make a feast and rejoice if we truly love her? Let us all rejoice, let us rejoice.

3. After Jesus Christ our Saviour had completed the work of our redemption by His death, the angels earnestly desired to have Our Lady with them in their heavenly country; hence they were continually supplicating Him, repeating the words of David, "Arise, oh Lord, into Your resting-place, You and the ark which You have sanctified." "Come, oh Lord, now that You have redeemed men, come to Your kingdom with us, and bring with You also the living ark of Your sanctification, namely, Your mother, who was the ark sanctified by You when You did inhabit her womb." At length, then, Our Lord wished to satisfy this desire of those citizens of the heavenly country, by calling Mary to paradise. But, if He wished that the ark of the covenant should be conducted with great pomp into the city of David with far more splendid and glorious pomp He ordained that His mother should enter into heaven. The prophet Elijah was carried up to heaven in a chariot of fire, which, according to the interpreters, was but a company of angels who raised him from the earth. But, to conduct you into heaven, oh mother of God a company of angels was not enough, but the King of heaven Himself, with all His celestial court, came to accompany you.

4. Jesus Christ, in order to honour the triumph of Mary, came Himself from paradise to meet and accompany her. And precisely for this object it was that the Redeemer wished to ascend before His mother, not only to prepare for her a throne in that palace, but also to render her entrance into heaven more glorious, accompanying her Himself, with all the blessed spirits. We shall find it more glorious than the Ascension of Jesus Christ; for the angels only came to

meet the Redeemer, but the Blessed Virgin went to glory met and accompanied by the Lord of glory Himself, and by all the blessed company of saints and angels. "I descended from heaven upon earth to give glory to My Father", The Lord said, "But afterwards, to pay honour to My mother, I ascended again into heaven, that I might thus be enabled to come to meet her, and accompany her by My presence to paradise."

5. Mary leaves the earth, and calling to mind the many graces she had there received from her Lord, she looks at it at the same time both with affection and compassion, leaving on it so many poor children, in the midst of so many miseries and dangers. And now Jesus offers her His hand, and the blessed mother rises in the air and passes beyond the clouds. Behold her now arrived at the gates of heaven. As at Our Lord's Ascension, now that Mary is going to take possession of the kingdom of the heavens, the angels who accompany her cry to the others who are within, "Lift up your gates, you princes, and be you lifted up, O eternal gates, and the queen of glory shall enter in."

6. And now Mary enters into the blessed country. But on her entrance, the celestial spirits seeing her so beautiful and glorious, ask of those who are without, "Who is this creature so beautiful, that comes from the desert of the earth, a place so full of thorns and tribulation? Who is she that comes so pure and so rich in virtue, supported by her beloved Lord, Who deigns to accompany her with so great honour?" The angels who accompany her answer, "This is the mother of our King, she is our queen, and the blessed one among women,

full of grace, the saint of saints, the beloved of God, the immaculate, the dove, the most beautiful of all creatures." And then all those blessed spirits begin to bless and praise her, singing, with more reason than the Hebrews said to Judith, "You are the glory of Jerusalem, you are the joy of Israel, you are the honour of our people. Ah! our Lady and our queen, then you are the glory of paradise, the joy of our country, you are the honour of us all; be ever welcome, be ever blessed; behold your kingdom, behold us, we are all your servants, ready for your commands."

7. Then all the saints who were at that time in paradise came to welcome her and salute her as their queen. All the holy virgins came. They saw her, and declared her most blessed and they praised her saying, "We are also queens of this kingdom, but you are our queen; for you were the first to give us the great example of consecrating our virginity to God; we all bless and thank you for it." Then came the holy confessors to salute her as their mistress, who had taught them so many beautiful virtues by her holy life. The holy martyrs came also to salute her as their queen, because by her great constancy in the sorrows of the passion of her son, she had taught them, and also obtained for them by her merits, strength to give their life for the faith. St. James came also, the only one of the apostles who was then in paradise, to thank her in the name of all the other apostles, for the great comfort and support she had given them while she was upon earth. The prophets next came to salute her, and they said to her, "Ah, Lady, you were foreshadowed in our prophecies." The holy patriarchs came and said to her, "Oh Mary, you have been our hope, so much and so long sighed

for by us." And among those came our first parents, Adam and Eve, to thank her with greater affection, "Ah, beloved daughter", they said to her, "You have repaired the injury done by us to the human race; you have obtained for the world that blessing lost by us, on account of our crime: by you we are saved, and for it be forever blessed."

8. Then came holy Simeon to kiss her feet, and with joy reminded her of that day on which he received from her hands the infant Jesus. St. Zechariah and St. Elizabeth also came, and thanked her again for that loving visit, that with so much humility and charity she made them in their dwelling, and through which they received so many treasures of grace. St. John the Baptist came with greater affection to thank her for having sanctified him by means of her voice. But what could her parents, St. Joachim and St. Ann, say to her, when they came to salute her? Oh God! with what tenderness must they have blessed her, saying, "Ah! beloved daughter, what happiness was ours in having such a child! Ah! be our queen now, because you are the mother of our God; as such we salute you and honour you." But who can comprehend the affection with which her dear spouse St. Joseph came to greet her? Who can describe the joy that the holy patriarch experienced at seeing his spouse arrive in heaven with so much triumph, made queen of all paradise? With what tenderness did he say to her, "Ah! my Lady and spouse, how shall I ever be able to thank our God as I ought for having made me your spouse, you who are His true mother? Through you I merited on earth to attend upon the childhood of the Incarnate Word, to bear Him so often in my arms, and receive from Him so many special favours.

Blessed be the moments that I spent in life serving Jesus and you, my holy spouse. Behold our Jesus; let us console ourselves that now He is no more lying in a stable upon hay, as we saw Him at His birth in Bethlehem; He does not now live poor and despised in a shop, as once He lived with us in Nazareth; He is not now nailed to a shameful cross, as when He died for the salvation of the world in Jerusalem; but He sits at the right hand of the Father, as king and Lord of heaven and of earth. And now, oh my queen, we shall never more depart from His holy feet, where we shall bless and love Him eternally."

9. Then all the angels came to salute her, and she, the great queen, thanked all for the assistance they had given her on earth, especially thanking the Archangel St. Gabriel, who was the happy ambassador of all her glories, when he came to announce to her that she was to be made Mother of God. Then the humble and holy Virgin, kneeling, adores the Divine Majesty, and wholly lost in the consciousness of her nothingness, thanks Him for all the graces bestowed upon her solely by His goodness, and especially for having made her mother of the Eternal Word. Let those who can, comprehend with what love the most holy Trinity blessed her. Let them comprehend what a welcome the eternal Father gave to His daughter, the Son to His mother, the Holy Spirit to His spouse. The Father crowns her by sharing with her His power, the Son His wisdom, the Holy Spirit His love. And all three Divine Persons establishing her throne at the right hand of Jesus, declare her universal queen of heaven and of earth, and command angels and all other creatures to recognise her for their queen, and as queen to serve and obey her.

10. Let us rejoice, then, with Mary, in the exalted throne to which God has elevated her in heaven. And let us rejoice also for our own sake, since if our mother has ceased to be present with us, by ascending in glory to heaven, she has not ceased to be present with us in her affection. Nay, being there nearer and more united to God, she better knows our miseries, and therefore pities them more, and is better able to relieve us. And will you, oh Blessed Virgin, because you have been so exalted in heaven, be forgetful of us miserable creatures? No, may God preserve us from the thought; a heart so merciful cannot but pity our miseries which are so great. If the pity of Mary for us was so great when she lived upon earth, much greater is it in heaven, where she reigns. Meanwhile let us dedicate ourselves to the service of this queen, to honour and love her as much as we can; for she is not, like other rulers, who oppress their vassals with burdens and taxes, but our queen enriches her servants with graces, merits, and rewards. Oh queen of heaven, you who sit so near to God, upon a throne so sublime, fill yourself with the glory of your Jesus, and send to us your servants the fragments that are left. You now enjoy the banquet of the Lord; we who are still on earth, like the dogs under the table, ask for your pity.

GLORY BE TO THE FATHER   Glory be to the Father, and to the Son, and to the Holy Spirit, as it was in the beginning, is now and ever shall be, world without end. Amen.

THE FATIMA PRAYER   O my Jesus, forgive us our sins, save us from the fires of hell, lead all souls to heaven, especially those in most need of Thy mercy.

CONCLUDING PRAYERS   *Upon completing the recitation of the Holy Rosary, the following prayers are customary, but others too may be added according to one's devotion and preference.*

HAIL HOLY QUEEN   Hail Holy Queen, Mother of Mercy, hail our life, our sweetness and our hope. To thee do we cry, poor banished children of Eve, to thee do we send up our sighs, mourning and weeping in this vale of tears. Turn then, most gracious advocate, thine eyes of mercy towards us, and after this, our exile, show unto us the blessed fruit of thy womb, Jesus. O clement, O loving, O sweet Virgin Mary. Pray for us O holy Mother of God, that we may be made worthy of the promises of Christ.

Let Us Pray   O God, Whose only begotten son, by His life, death and resurrection, has purchased for us the rewards of eternal life, grant we beseech You, that meditating on these mysteries of the most Holy Rosary of the Blessed Virgin Mary, we may both imitate what they contain and obtain what they promise, through the same Christ our Lord. Amen.

PRAYER TO SAINT MICHAEL THE ARCHANGEL   Holy Michael, the Archangel, defend us in the day of battle. Be our safeguard against the wickedness and snares of the devil. May God rebuke him, we humbly pray; and do thou, O Prince of the heavenly hosts, by the power of God thrust down into hell Satan and all the evil spirits who wander through the world seeking the ruin of souls. Amen.

MEMORARE   Remember, O most gracious Virgin Mary, that never was it known that anyone who fled to thy protection, implored thy help, or sought thine intercession was left unaided. Inspired by this confidence, I fly unto thee, O Virgin of virgins, my mother; to thee do I come, before you I stand, sinful and sorrowful. O Mother of the Word Incarnate, despise not my petitions, but in thy mercy hear and answer me. Amen.

May the Divine Assistance remain always with us, and may the souls of the faithful departed, through the mercy of God rest in peace. Amen.

The Mysteries of Light

The Baptism of Our Lord in the River Jordan

Gratitude for the gift of Holy baptism which begins the Life of Grace

UR LOVING REDEEMER DESIRES from the very beginning to communicate to us the grace of Redemption, and therefore He begins to make Himself known even to the Gentiles, who neither knew Him nor looked for His coming. O Saviour of the world, what would have happened to us if You had not come to enlighten us? We should be like our forefathers, who worshipped as gods, animals, stones, and wood, and consequently we should have all been damned. I give You thanks on behalf of all the baptised, and those who have benefited from Your redemption.

OUR FATHER   Our Father, Who art in Heaven, hallowed be Thy name, Thy kingdom come, Thy will be done, on earth as it is in heaven. Give us this day our daily bread; and forgive us our trespasses, as we forgive those who trespass against us; and lead us not into temptation, but deliver us from evil. Amen.

HAIL MARY (10)   Hail Mary, Full of Grace, the Lord is with thee. Blessed art thou among women and blessed is the fruit of thy womb, Jesus. Holy Mary, Mother of God, pray for us sinners now, and at the hour of our death. Amen.

1. The Baptist, when he showed to the Jews that their Messiah was already come, said, "Behold the Lamb of God, Who takes away the sin of the world." Jesus wishes to be seen as a lamb, and above all other virtues, meekness is the virtue of the lamb. It is also the special virtue of Our Saviour, Who says, "Learn of Me, because I am meek and humble of heart." He showed the extent of His meekness in doing good to the ungrateful, in submitting sweetly to His enemies, and in bearing without complaint all that insulted and maltreated Him, "When He was reviled, did not revile in return, when He suffered, He threatened not, but delivered Himself to him who judged Him unjustly."

After being scourged, crowned with thorns, covered with spittle, nailed to a cross, and saturated with opprobrium, He forgot all, and prayed for those that had thus maltreated Him. Hence He has exhorted us, above all things, to learn from His example humility and meekness.

2. Meekness is, of all virtues, that which renders us most like to God. Yes, for it belongs only to God to render good for evil. Meekness consists not in being agreeable to the meek, but in treating with sweetness those that know not what meekness is. When a neighbour is enraged there is no better means of appeasing his anger than by answering with sweetness. As water extinguishes fire, so, a mild answer softens the anger of a brother. Even towards sinners the most abandoned, obstinate, and insolent we must exercise all possible meekness in order to draw them to God. David said, "The meek shall inherit the land, and shall delight in abundance of peace." Nothing is able to disturb their serenity. No insult, no loss, no misfortune, disturbs the peace of a meek heart. The meek are dear to God and to men. There is nothing that gives greater edification to others, and draws souls more powerfully to God, than the meekness of the man who, when treated with derision, contempt, and insult, seeks not revenge, but bears all with a peaceful and placid countenance. Moses was more beloved by the Hebrews on account of the meekness with which he received insults, than on account of the miracles which He wrought. "Learn of Me, because I am meek and humble of heart", "Behold the Lamb of God."

3. When there is question of the Divine honour, we should not be frightened by the dignity of the man who offends God; let us say to him openly, "That is sinful; it cannot be done". Let us imitate St. John the Baptist who reproved King Herod for living with his brother's wife, and said to him, "It is not lawful for you to have her." Men, indeed, will regard us as fools, and turn us into derision; but on the Day of Judgment they will acknowledge that they have been fools, and we shall have the glory of being numbered among the Saints.

4. Oh, how just God is when the time of vengeance arrives! He causes the sinner to be ensnared and strangled in the net his own hands have woven. Such was the case for Herodias, who had caused St. John the Baptist to be beheaded. As she was crossing frozen water one day the ice broke under her, and she remained with her head above the ice. In her violent struggling for life, her head was severed from her body, and thus she died. Let us tremble when we see others punished, knowing as we do, that we ourselves have deserved the same punishments. Give ear to the words of the saintly Baptist, "For now the axe is laid to the root of the trees." When the tree is felled from the root, it dies and is cast into the fire. The Lord stands with the scourge in His hand. Let sin be no more for us, my brethren, let us be converted and escape the scourge which hangs over us.

5. All would wish to be saved and to enjoy the glory of Paradise; but to gain Heaven, it is necessary to walk in the straight road that leads to eternal bliss. This road is the observance of the divine commands. Hence, in his

preaching, the Baptist exclaimed, "Make straight the way of the Lord." In order to be able to walk always in the way of the Lord, without turning to the right or to the left, it is necessary to adopt the proper means. These means are, first, diffidence in ourselves; secondly, confidence in God; thirdly, resistance to temptations.

6. Through the holy sacrament of baptism the Christian's tongue has been consecrated to God. On the tongue of all who are baptised is placed blessed salt, that their tongues may be made sacred, and may be accustomed to bless God. How wicked that the blasphemer afterwards makes his tongue a sword to pierce the heart of God. No sin contains in itself so much malice as the sin of blasphemy. Moreover blasphemies against the saints or against holy things such as the sacraments are of the same species as blasphemies against God for it is God Who is the foundation of their sanctity. Have ready on your tongue good words, rather then impatient blasphemies. Through the holy sacrament of baptism your tongue has been consecrated to God.

7. So great was the love which inflamed the enamoured heart of Jesus, that He not only wished to die for our redemption, but during His whole life He sighed ardently for the day on which He should suffer death for the love of us. Hence, during His life, Jesus used to say, "I have a baptism wherewith I am to be baptised; and how am I straitened until it be accomplished", that is "How greatly I desire My passion, in which I am to be baptised with the baptism of My own blood, in order to wash away the sins of men."

8. Whoever is baptised enters into the state of grace and is the friend of God. He also becomes an adopted son of God. This is the great gift which we have received from the divine love of Jesus Christ at baptism. "Behold", says St. John, "what manner of charity the Father has bestowed upon us, that we should be called, and should be, the sons of God." The soul is now the temple of the Holy Spirit, indeed, a saintly religious sister saw a devil go out from an infant who was receiving Baptism and the Holy Spirit enter with a multitudes of angels.

9. Alas! My soul also was once beautiful, when it received Your grace in Baptism; but I have disfigured it since by my sins; You alone, my Redeemer, can restore it to its former beauty. Do this by Your Passion, and then do with me what You will.

10. It is appointed. It is certain, then, that we are all condemned to death. We are born with the halter round the neck, and every step we make brings us nearer to death. As in speaking of those who have already departed you say, "God be merciful to my father, to my uncle, to my brother", so others shall say the same of you. As your name was one day inserted in the Register of Baptisms, so it shall be one day written in the records of the dead.

GLORY BE TO THE FATHER   Glory be to the Father, and to the Son, and to the Holy Spirit, as it was in the beginning, is now and ever shall be, world without end. Amen.

THE FATIMA PRAYER   O my Jesus, forgive us our sins, save us from the fires of hell, lead all souls to heaven, especially those in most need of Thy mercy.

The Miracle at the Wedding Feast of Cana

THE FRUIT OF THIS MYSTERY

Humility in prayer

HE TENDERNESS OF MARY'S Mercy is made manifest at Cana. The wine fails, the spouses are troubled, no one speaks to Mary to ask her son to console them in their necessity. But the tenderness of Mary's heart which cannot but pity the afflicted, moved her to take the office of advocate, and without being asked, to entreat her son to work a miracle. Unasked, she assumed the office of an advocate and a compassionate helper. If, unasked, this good Lady has done so much, what will she not do for those who invoke her intercession?

OUR FATHER   Our Father, Who art in Heaven, hallowed be Thy name, Thy kingdom come, Thy will be done, on earth as it is in heaven. Give us this day our daily bread; and forgive us our trespasses, as we forgive those who trespass against us; and lead us not into temptation, but deliver us from evil. Amen.

HAIL MARY (10)   Hail Mary, Full of Grace, the Lord is with thee. Blessed art thou among women and blessed is the fruit of thy womb, Jesus. Holy Mary, Mother of God, pray for us sinners now, and at the hour of our death. Amen.

1. Our Lady is so full of mercy, that, as soon as she sees misery, she instantly obtains relief, and cannot behold any one in distress without coming to his assistance. Indeed, she anticipates our supplications, and obtains aid for us before we ask her prayers. It was thus she acted when she lived on this earth, as we learn from what happened at the marriage of Cana in Galilee; where, when, the wine failed, she did not wait to be asked, but taking pity on the affliction and shame of the spouses, asked her son to console them, saying, "They have no wine."

2. At the nuptials of Cana, Mary, informing her son that wine that was lacking, said, "They have no wine;" Jesus answered, "Woman, what is that to Me and to you? My

hour is not yet come." But although the time for miracles has not yet arrived, our Saviour, in order to obey His mother, performed the miracle she requested, and converted the water into wine.

3. St. Paul exhorts us, "Let us go therefore with confidence to the throne of grace; that we may obtain mercy, and find grace in seasonable aid." The throne of grace is the Blessed Virgin Mary. If, then, we wish for graces, let us go to the throne of grace, which is Mary; and let us go with the hope of being certainly heard; for we have the intercession of Mary, who obtains whatever she asks for. The Holy Spirit, filling the Blessed Virgin with all His sweetness, has rendered her so dear to God that everyone who, through her intercession, asked for graces, will certainly obtain them.

4. Mary, as if Jesus had already granted her the favour, said to the attendants, "Fill the water-pots with water"; and Jesus Christ, indeed to please His mother, changed that water into the best wine. But how is this? If the time appointed for miracles was the time of preaching, how could it be anticipated by the miracle of the wine, contrary to the divine decree? Nothing, it may be answered, was done contrary to the divine decree; for although, generally speaking, the time for signs had not come, yet from eternity God had established by another general decree, that nothing the divine mother could ask should ever be denied her.

5. Mary, well acquainted with her privilege, although her son seemed to have then set aside her petition, said notwithstanding, that the water-pots should be filled, as though the

favour was already granted. Moreover, Jesus Christ wished to show that He would have deferred the miracle, if another had asked Him to perform it; but because His mother asked it, He immediately performed it.

6. It is related of Coriolanus, that when he held Rome besieged, all the prayers of his friends and of the citizens could not induce him to withdraw his forces; but when his mother Veturia came to entreat him he could not resist, and immediately stopped the siege. But the prayers of Mary are as much more powerful with Jesus than the prayers of Veturia with her son, as the love and gratitude of Jesus to Mary exceeds that of the Son of Veturia for his mother. One sigh of Mary has more power than the prayers of all the saints united. The devil himself confessed this same thing to St. Dominic, when, constrained by his commands, he spoke through the mouth of a possessed person, that one sigh of Mary availed more with God than the united prayers of all the saints.

7. Oh truly immense and admirable goodness of God, Who to us miserable, guilty creatures, has granted you, oh our Lady, for our advocate, that you might, by your powerful intercession, obtain for us whatever good You will. Oh, the great mercy of God, Who, that we might not flee to hide ourselves from the sentence to be pronounced upon us, has destined His own mother and the treasurer of graces to be our advocate.

8. God gave us the Virgin Mary as an example of all virtues, but especially as an example of patience. At the nuptials of

Cana Jesus Christ gave an answer to the most holy Virgin, by which He seemed to pay but little regard to her prayers. Precisely for this reason, that He might give us an example of the patience of His holy mother. The whole life of Mary was a continual exercise of patience, for, as an angel revealed to St. Bridget, the blessed Virgin lived always in the midst of sufferings and yet persevered most faithfully in carrying out God's holy will.

9. Persuaded by the prayers of His mother the Lord gives. Jesus cannot but graciously hear Mary in all her petitions, wishing in this, as it were, to obey her as His true mother. He also grants her petitions in order to thank her, inasmuch as she gave to Him of herself a true human nature. The prayers of Mary, therefore, have a certain authority with Jesus Christ, and so she obtains pardon even for the greatest sinners when they commend themselves to her.

10. The Virgin said one day to St. Bridget that miserable, and miserable for eternity, shall be the sinner who, though he has it in his power during life to come to her who is able and willing to assist him, neglects to invoke her aid, and is lost. "The devil", says St. Peter, "goes about as a roaring lion seeking whom he may devour." But this Mother of Mercy constantly goes about in search of sinners to save them. This Queen of clemency presents our petitions, and begins to assist us before we ask the assistance of her prayers. Because Mary's heart is so full of tenderness towards us that she cannot behold our miseries without affording relief. Let us, then, in all our wants, be most careful to have recourse to this Mother of Mercy who is always ready to assist those

who invoke her aid. She is always prepared to come to our help and frequently anticipates our supplications; but ordinarily, she requires that we should pray to her, and is offended when we neglect to ask her assistance.

GLORY BE TO THE FATHER   Glory be to the Father, and to the Son, and to the Holy Spirit, as it was in the beginning, is now and ever shall be, world without end. Amen.

THE FATIMA PRAYER   O my Jesus, forgive us our sins, save us from the fires of hell, lead all souls to heaven, especially those in most need of Thy mercy.

The Proclamation of the Kingdom and the Call to Conversion

AFTER THIRTY YEARS OF hidden life, finally the time comes for our Saviour to appear in public to preach His heavenly doctrines, which He had come from heaven to teach us; and therefore it was necessary that He should make Himself known as the true Son of God. But, O my God! how many were there that acknowledge and honoured Him as He deserved? Besides the few disciples who followed Him, all the rest, instead of honouring Him, despised Him as a vile man and an impostor. Jesus Christ was contradicted and despised by all: He was despised in His doctrine; for when He declared that He was the only-begotten Son of God, He was called a blasphemer, and as such was condemned to death. He was despised in His wisdom; for He was esteemed a fool without sense. He was accused of being a sorcerer, and of having commerce with devils. He was called a heretic, and one possessed by the devil. In fine, Jesus Christ was considered by all the people so wicked a man that there was no need of a tribunal to condemn Him to be crucified. Jesus Christ, by choosing for His holy ministry such derision, and receiving so ignominious a death, has ennobled and taken away all bitterness from contempt and opprobrium. It is for this that the saints in this world were always so fond and even desirous of being despised.

OUR FATHER   Our Father, Who art in Heaven, hallowed be Thy name, Thy kingdom come, Thy will be done, on earth as it is in heaven. Give us this day our daily bread; and forgive us our trespasses, as we forgive those who trespass against us; and lead us not into temptation, but deliver us from evil. Amen.

HAIL MARY (10)   Hail Mary, Full of Grace, the Lord is with thee. Blessed art thou among women and blessed is the fruit of thy womb, Jesus. Holy Mary, Mother of God, pray for us sinners now, and at the hour of our death. Amen.

1. Our Saviour desired that His disciples, although He had destined them to propagate the faith by journeying

through the whole world, from time to time should leave their labours, and retire to solitude, to commune with God alone. Besides, let us remember that Jesus Christ, from the time when He began to live with the world, was accustomed to send them into the different parts of Judea, that they might convert sinners; but, after their labours, He did not cease to call them to retire to some solitary place. If our Lord said, even to the Apostles, "Rest a while," it is indeed necessary for all holy labourers to retire, from time to time, into solitude, to preserve their recollectedness with God, and to obtain strength to labour with greater vigour for the salvation of souls. Certainly, Jesus Christ did not mean by this expression that the Apostles were to set themselves to slumber, but that they should repose in holding communion with God, in praying to Him for the graces necessary for living well, and thus should gain strength for conducting the salvation of souls, for without this rest with God in prayer, strength fails for labouring rightly to our own benefit, and to the profit of others. Certainly, holy solitude is always to be loved, even if it cannot always be obtained; those called by God to the conversion of sinners cannot remain always shut up in a cell, for doing so would violate their divine calling. Yet, nevertheless, they should never cease to sigh for solitude, and take advantage of it whenever God allows it to them.

2. The works of Martha, without the recollection of Mary, cannot be perfect. He deceives himself, who expects, without the aid of prayer, to succeed in the work of saving souls a work as dangerous as it is sublime; without the reflection of mental prayer, he shall certainly faint on the way. Our

Lord commanded His disciples to preach what they heard in prayer, "That which you hear in the ear, preach from the housetops." That is, the ear of the heart, to which God promises to speak in the solitude of prayer. Each Christian should be first a reservoir, that is, full of holy lights and affections collected in prayer, and afterwards a channel to diffuse them among his neighbours. Alas in the Church today, there are many who would be channels and few who would be reservoirs. That a Christian may be able to draw many souls to God, he must first prepare himself to be drawn by God. Such has been the conduct of holy workmen in Gods vineyard of St. Dominic, St. Philip Neri, St. Francis Xavier, St. John Francis Regis. They employed the day in labouring for the people, and spent the night in prayer, and persevered in that holy exercise until they were overcome by sleep. A person of moderate learning and great zeal will bring more souls to God than a great number of tepid though learned individuals. A single word from a Christian inflamed with holy charity will do more good than a hundred sermons composed by a theologian who has but little love of God.

3. The Lord justly complains that many Christians are deficient to Him by neglecting to ask His graces. Of this precisely the Redeemer appears to have complained one day to His disciples, "Up to now you have not asked anything in My name; ask and you shall receive, that your joy may be full" As if He said, "Do not complain of Me if you do not enjoy complete happiness; complain of yourselves for not having asked My graces: ask Me for them henceforth, and you shall be satisfied." Hence in their conferences, the ancient monks came to the conclusion, that there is no

exercise more conducive to salvation than to pray always and say, "O Lord, come to my aid, O Lord make haste to help me." We have a God Who loves us to excess, and Who is solicitous for our salvation, and therefore He is always ready to hear all who ask His graces. The princes of the earth give audience only to a few; but God gives audience to all who wish for it.

4. Our Redeemer declares that He came down from heaven for the very end of preaching the Gospel. Indeed, He sought no other proof of Peter's love for Him but this, that he should procure the salvation of souls. That is He did not impose upon him penance, prayers, or other things, but only that he should endeavour to feed and tend His sheep. What greater glory then can any man have than to be a co-operator with God in this great work of the salvation of souls? He who loves the Lord ardently is not content to be alone in loving Him, he would draw all to His love, saying with David, "O magnify the Lord with me, together let us extol His name." The man who labours for the salvation of souls with true zeal has great grounds for hoping in his own salvation, as St. Augustine says, "Have you saved a soul? Then you have predestinated your own."

5. Jesus Christ has made priests, as it were, His co-operators in procuring the honour of His Eternal Father and the salvation of souls, and therefore, when He ascended into heaven, He protested that He left them to hold His place, and to continue the work of redemption which He had undertaken and consummated, saying to His disciples, "I leave you to perform the very office for which I came into

the world; that is, to make known to men the name of My Father." And addressing His Eternal Father, He said, concerning His priests, "I have given them Your word. Sanctify them in the truth." And so priests are placed in the world to make known to men God and His perfections, His justice and mercy, His commands, and to procure the respect, obedience, and love that He deserves. Priests are are appointed to seek the lost sheep, and when necessary, to give their lives for them. In every government ministers are appointed to enforce the observance of the laws, to remove scandals, to repress the seditious, and to defend the honour of the king. For all these ends the Lord has constituted priests the officers of His court. The sacerdotal dignity surpasses even the dignity of the angels, for all the angels in heaven cannot absolve from a single sin. Who is it that has an arm like the arm of God, and thunders with a voice like the thundering voice of God? It is the priest, who, in giving absolution, exerts the arm and voice of God, by which He rescues souls from Hell. The priest holds the place of Christ, he is Christ's servant, working with Him in procuring the salvation of souls.

6. The Lord Jesus, having gone up into one of the ships, and having heard from St. Peter, that he and his companions had laboured all the night and had taken nothing, said to the disciples, "Launch out into the deep, and let down your nets for a draught." They obeyed; and having cast out their nets into the sea, they took such a multitude of fish, that the nets were nearly broken. Brethren, God has placed us in the midst of the sea of this life, and has commanded us to cast out our nets, that we may catch fish; that is, that we

may perform good works, by which we can acquire merits for eternal life.

7. The Lord, having gone up into a mountain with His disciples, and seeing a multitude of five thousand persons, who followed Him because they saw the miracles which He wrought on them that were diseased, said to St. Philip, "From where shall we buy bread, that these may eat?" "Lord," answered St. Philip, "Two-hundred pounds of bread would not be sufficient for every one to take even a little." St. Andrew then said, "There is a boy here that has five barley loaves and two fish; but what are these among so many?" But Jesus Christ said, "Make the men sit down." And He distributed the loaves and fishes among them. The multitude were satisfied, and the fragments of bread which remained filled twelve baskets. The Lord wrought this miracle through compassion for the bodily wants of these poor people; but far more tender is His compassion for the necessities of the souls of the poor, that is, of sinners who are deprived of the divine grace.

8. The Lord declared His tenderness towards penitent sinners in the parable of the Prodigal Son. In that parable the Son of God describes a certain young man, the figure of a sinner, who, after departing from God, and losing the divine grace and all the merits he had acquired, leads a life of misery under the slavery of the devil. The young man, seeing his wretched condition, resolved to return to his father, the figure of Jesus Christ. The father, seeing His son return to Him, was instantly moved to pity, and, instead of driving him away, as the ungrateful son had deserved,

ran with open arms to meet him, and, through tenderness, fell upon his neck, and consoled him by His embraces. He then tells the servants to bring "the first robe" signifying the divine grace, which, in addition to new celestial gifts, God, by granting pardon, gives to the penitent sinner. By recovering the grace of God, the soul becomes again the spouse of Jesus Christ, signified by the ring the father gives him. The fatted calf which they celebrate with signifies the holy communion, or Jesus in the holy sacrament mystically killed and offered in sacrifice on the altar. Let us eat and rejoice. "But why, O Lord Jesus, so much joy at the return of so ungrateful a child?" Because, answers the father, "This My son was dead, and he is come to life again; he was lost, and I have found him."

9. This tenderness of Jesus Christ was experienced by the sinful woman, Mary Magdalene, who cast herself at the feet of Jesus, and washed them with her tears. The Lord, turning to her with sweetness, consoled her by saying, "Daughter, your sins are pardoned; Your confidence in Me has saved you; go in peace." This tenderness was also felt by the man who was sick for thirty-eight years, and who was infirm both in body and soul. The Lord cured his malady, and pardoned his sins. The Redeemer encourages us to throw ourselves at His feet with a secure hope of consolation and pardon. "Come to Me, all you that labour and are burdened, and I will refresh you", that is, "Come to Me, all you poor sinners, who labour for your own damnation, and groan under the weight of your crimes; come, and I will deliver you from all your troubles." Let us then, O sinners, return instantly to Jesus Christ. If we have left Him, let us immediately

return, before death overtakes us in sin and sends us to hell, where the mercies and graces of the Lord shall, if we do not amend, be so many swords which shall lacerate the heart for all eternity.

10. One day, the Pharisees, with the malignant intention of ensnaring the Lord in His speech, that they might afterwards accuse Him before the ministers of Caesar, sent their disciples to ask Jesus Christ, if it were lawful to pay tribute to Caesar. In answer, the Redeemer, after looking at the coin of the tribute, asked, "Whose image and inscription is this?" Being told it was Caesar's, He said, "Render then to Caesar the things that are Caesar's, and to God the things that are God's." By these words Jesus Christ wishes to teach us, that it is our duty to give to men what is due to them; and to reserve for Him all the affections of our heart, since He created us to love Him. Miserable the man who, at the hour of death, shall see that he has loved creatures, that he has loved his pleasures, and has not loved God. Behold, the unhappy man shall then say, first, "O God! I could have become a saint, but have not become one." Secondly, he shall say, "Oh! that I now had time to repair the evil I have done! But time is at an end." Thirdly, "Oh! that at least, in the short time which remains, I could remedy the past: but, alas! this time is not fit for repairing past evils."

GLORY BE TO THE FATHER   Glory be to the Father, and to the Son, and to the Holy Spirit, as it was in the beginning, is now and ever shall be, world without end. Amen.

THE FATIMA PRAYER   O my Jesus, forgive us our sins, save us from the fires of hell, lead all souls to heaven, especially those in most need of Thy mercy.

The Transfiguration of the Lord on Mount Tabor

THE FRUIT OF THIS MYSTERY

A holy disdain for the pleasures of this passing world

AVISHED WITH JOY AND delight, St. Peter exclaimed, "Lord, it is good for us to be here." That is, "Lord, let us remain here; let us never more depart from this place; for, the sight of Your beauty consoles us more than all the delights of the earth." The Lord wished to give His disciples a glimpse of the glory of Paradise, in order to animate them to labour for the Divine Honour. And so, brethren, let us labour during the remainder of our lives to gain heaven.

OUR FATHER   Our Father, Who art in Heaven, hallowed be Thy name, Thy kingdom come, Thy will be done, on earth as it is in heaven. Give us this day our daily bread; and forgive us our trespasses, as we forgive those who trespass against us; and lead us not into temptation, but deliver us from evil. Amen.

HAIL MARY (10)   Hail Mary, Full of Grace, the Lord is with thee. Blessed art thou among women and blessed is the fruit of thy womb, Jesus. Holy Mary, Mother of God, pray for us sinners now, and at the hour of our death. Amen.

1. When the Redeemer was transfigured, He allowed the disciples to behold the splendour of His countenance, and the joys of heaven. Heaven is so great a good, that, to purchase it for us, Jesus Christ has sacrificed His life on the cross. Be assured that the greatest of all the torments of the damned in hell, arises from the thought of having lost heaven through their own fault. The blessings, the delights, the joys, the sweetness of Paradise can be described and understood only by those blessed souls that enjoy them.

2. According to the Apostle, no man on this earth can comprehend the infinite blessings which God has prepared for the souls that love Him. In this life we cannot have an idea of any other pleasures than those which we enjoy by means of the senses. Perhaps we imagine that the beauty of heaven

resembles that of a wide extended plain covered with the verdure of spring, interspersed with trees in full bloom, and abounding in birds fluttering about and singing on every side; or, that it is like the beauty of a garden full of fruits and flowers, and surrounded by fountains in continual play. What a joy to behold such a plain, or such a garden! But, oh! how much greater are the beauties of heaven!

3. A great saint once exclaimed, full of amazement and love, "First, I see my Saviour in heaven between the Father and the Holy Spirit; Then I see Him upon the Mount Tabor, between two saints, Moses and Elijah; how, then, can I see Him crucified upon Calvary between two thieves?" Let us not, then, cease, O devout souls, ever to keep before our eyes Jesus crucified, and dying in the midst of torments and insults through love of us.

4. We cannot have a more powerful motive for loving God than the Passion of Jesus Christ, by which we know that the Eternal Father, to manifest to us His exceeding love for us, was pleased to send His only begotten son upon earth to die for us sinners. This was precisely the expression used by Moses and Elijah on Mount Tabor, in speaking of the Passion of Jesus Christ. They did not know how to give it any other description than an 'excess' of love, as Scripture recalls, "They spoke of His excess, which He should consummate in Jerusalem."

5. The Holy prophets on Mount Tabor spoke truly when they called the death of Jesus Christ an "excess", for it was an excess of suffering and of love, so much so that it would

be impossible to believe it, if it had not already happened. To this end the Son of God wished to come on earth, to live a life so laborious and to die a death so bitter, namely, that He might make known to man how much He loved him. How many youths, how many noblemen, are there not, who have left their house, their country, their riches, their parents, and all, to retire into cloisters, to live only for the love of Jesus Christ! How many young virgins, renouncing their nuptials with princes and the great ones of the world, have gone with joyfulness to death, to render thus some compensation for the love of a God who had been executed on an infamous gibbet, and died for their sake!

6. A Holy Martyr, before his wicked judge, cried out in faith, "There is an eternal light incalculably better than this world, which in a short time must, to us, be obscured forever! Happiness which never ends is, without comparison, preferable to that which shortly terminates; and is it prudent to prefer eternal enjoyments to those that quickly fail?"

7. The law of Jesus Christ commands us to battle against our inordinate inclinations, to love our enemies, to mortify our body, to be patient in adversities and to place all our hope in the life to come. But all this does not make the life of the truly faithful a sad and sorrowful one. The religion of Jesus Christ says to us, as it were, "Come and unite yourselves to Me; I will lead you along a mountain path which to the bodily eyes seems rough and hard to climb, but to those of good will is easy and agreeable."

8. Who will give me the wings of the dove to fly to my God, and, divested of all earthly affection, to repose in the bosom of the divinity? Holy desires are the blessed wings with which the saints burst every worldly tie, and fly to the mountain of perfection, where they find that peace which the world cannot give. A man who is desirous of obtaining a valuable treasure which he knows is to be found at the top of a lofty mountain, but who, through fear of fatigue and difficulty, has no desire of ascending, will never advance a single step towards the treasure, but will remain below. In seeking eternal salvation, we must, according to St. Paul, never rest, but must run continually in the way of perfection, that we may win the prize.

9. You seek peace and pleasure? Well and good! Which peace is to be preferred? That which, when scarcely tasted, disappears and leaves the heart replete with bitterness, or that which will rejoice and satiate you for all eternity? You strive for honours? Very well! Which do you prefer, that empty honour that disappears like a puff of smoke, or that true and genuine honour which will one day glorify you before the whole world? Ask those who lead a life of faith if the renunciation of this world's goods makes them sad! Visit the holy hermit in his grotto, or the devoted sister in her convent and ask them if they miss the joys and pleasures of this earth! They will answer without hesitation, 'No, no; we desire but God alone and nothing else.'"

10. The path of the just is as a shining light going forwards and increasing even to perfect day. The way of the wicked is obscure and shadowed, and they may fall down at any

point. As light increases constantly from sunrise to full day, so the path of the saints always advances; but the way of sinners becomes continually more dark and gloomy, they know not where they go, until finally they stumble off the precipice, into eternity.

GLORY BE TO THE FATHER   Glory be to the Father, and to the Son, and to the Holy Spirit, as it was in the beginning, is now and ever shall be, world without end. Amen.

THE FATIMA PRAYER   O my Jesus, forgive us our sins, save us from the fires of hell, lead all souls to heaven, especially those in most need of Thy mercy.

The Institution of the Holy Eucharist

THE FRUIT OF THIS MYSTERY

The resolution to make frequent visits to the Blessed Sacrament

 N NO OTHER ACTION can the Saviour be considered more tender or more loving than in the institution of the Holy Eucharist; in which He, as it were, annihilates Himself, and becomes food, in order to penetrate our souls, and to unite Himself to the hearts of His faithful servants. Thus, we are united with that Lord

on Whom the angels dare not fix their eyes, and are made
one flesh. What shepherd, has ever fed His sheep with His
own blood? Jesus, in the sacrament, nourishes us with His
own blood, and unites us to Himself. And why become
our food? Because, He loved us ardently, and by making
Himself our food, He wished to unite Himself entirely to
us, and to make Himself one thing with us. Jesus Christ
wished to perform the greatest of His miracles in order to
satisfy His desire of remaining with us, and of uniting in
one, our heart and His own most holy heart. O wonderful
is Your love, O Lord Jesus! You wished to incorporate us
in such a manner with Yourself, that we should have one
heart and one soul inseparably united to You.

OUR FATHER   Our Father, Who art in Heaven, hallowed
be Thy name, Thy kingdom come, Thy will be done, on
earth as it is in heaven. Give us this day our daily bread; and
forgive us our trespasses, as we forgive those who trespass
against us; and lead us not into temptation, but deliver us
from evil. Amen.

HAIL MARY (10)   Hail Mary, Full of Grace, the Lord is
with thee. Blessed art thou among women and blessed is
the fruit of thy womb, Jesus. Holy Mary, Mother of God,
pray for us sinners now, and at the hour of our death. Amen.

1. My soul, behold your Jesus, rising from the table, laying
aside His garments, taking a white cloth and girding Himself
with it. He afterwards puts water into a basin, kneels down
before His disciples, and begins to wash their feet. Then
the sovereign of the universe, the only-begotten of God,

humbles Himself so as to wash the feet of His creatures. O angels, what do you say? It would have been a great favour if Jesus Christ had permitted them, as He did Magdalene, to wash His divine feet with their tears. But no; He wished to place Himself at the feet of His servants in order to leave us at the end of His life this great example of humility, and this proof of the great love that He bears to men. And, O Lord, shall we be always so proud as not to be able to bear a word of contempt, or the smallest inattention, without instantly feeling resentment, and thinking of seeking revenge, after we had by our sins deserved to be trampled on by the devils in hell? Ah, my Jesus, Your example has rendered humiliations and insults amiable to us. I purpose henceforth to bear every injury and affront for the love of You.

2. Knowing that the time of His death and departure from this world had come, and having hitherto loved men even to excess, He wished to give them the last and the greatest proof of His love. Behold Him seated at table, all on fire with charity, turning to His disciples and saying, "With desire I have desired to eat this Pasch with you." That is, "My disciples, know that I have desired nothing during My whole life but to eat this last supper with you; for after it I Shall go to sacrifice My life for your salvation." Happy You, O beloved John, who, leaning Your head on the bosom of Jesus, did then understand the tenderness of the love of this loving Redeemer for the souls that love Him! Ah my sweet Lord, You have frequently favoured me with a similar grace. Yes, I too have felt the tenderness of Your affection for me, when You consoled me with celestial lights and spiritual sweetness; but, after all Your favours, I have not

been faithful to You. Ah, do not permit me to live any longer ungrateful to Your goodness. I wish to be all Yours, accept me and assist me.

3. The Lord Jesus, the same night on which He was betrayed, took bread, and, giving thanks, broke it, saying, "Take this all of you and eat of it, for this is My Body." At the very time that men prepared for Him scourges, thorns and a cross to crucify Him, the loving Saviour wished to leave us this the last proof of His love. And why at death, and not before that time, did He institute this sacrament? Because, the marks of love given by friends at death make a greater impression on the memory, and are preserved with greater affection. Jesus Christ had already given Himself to us in many ways, He had given Himself to us for a companion, a master, a father; for our light and our victim. The last degree of love remained; and this was, to give Himself to us for our food in order to untie Himself entirely to us, as food is united with Him who eats it. This He has done by giving Himself to us in the Most Holy Sacrament. Thus, our Redeemer was not content with uniting Himself only to our human nature: He wished by this sacrament to find a means of also uniting Himself to each of us in particular.

4. The Redeemer wished to give Himself to us under the appearance of bread, that all might be able to receive Him. Had He given Himself to us under the appearance of costly food, the poor would not be able to receive Him, and had He instituted the Holy Sacrament under the appearance of any other cheap food, this perhaps would not be found in all parts of the world. Jesus wished to leave Himself under

the species of bread, because it costs but little, and is found in every country; so that all persons in all places may find Him and receive Him. Moreover, He endeavours to allure us to the holy table by promises to eternal life saying, "He that eats My flesh and drinks My blood, has life everlasting." He also threatens to exclude from paradise all who neglect to receive Him in the holy sacrament, "Except you eat the flesh of the Son of man, and drink His blood, you shall not have life in you." These invitations, promises, and threats all proceed from the ardent desire of Jesus Christ to unite Himself to us in this sacrament. And this desire springs from the great love which He bears us; for, the end of love is nothing else than to be united with the object of love. Our Lord said one day to St Mechtilde, "The bee does not cast itself on the flower from which it sucks the honey, with as much ardour as I come to the soul that desires to receive Me."

5. Go forth again, and behold Him, your spouse, all full of compassion and love, now that He comes to unite Himself to you in this sacrament of love. Has it indeed, then, cost You so much, my beloved Jesus, before You could come and unite Yourself to souls in this most sweet Sacrament? Were You indeed obliged to suffer so bitter and ignominious a death? Oh, come, then, without delay, and unite Yourself to my soul also. It was at one time Your enemy by sin; but now You desire to espouse it by Your grace. Come, O Jesus, my spouse, for never more will I betray You; I am determined to be ever faithful to You. As a loving spouse, my whole thought shall be to find out Your pleasure. I am determined to love You without reserve; I desire to be all Yours, my Jesus, all, all, all.

6. That great servant of God, Fr. De la Colombière, used to say, "If anything could shake my faith in the mystery of the Eucharist, I would not doubt of the power, but rather of the love, which God displays in this sacrament. If you ask me how bread becomes the body of Jesus or how Jesus is found in many places, I answer that God can do all things. But if you ask me how it is that God loves men so as to make Himself their food, I can only say that I do not understand it, and that the love of Jesus cannot be comprehended." St Bernard's answer is that love makes lovers forget their own dignity. Love seeks not what is convenient when there is question of making itself known to the beloved; it goes not where it ought, but where it is carried by the ardour of its desire. Justly, then, has the angelic Doctor called this sacrament "a sacrament of love, a pledge of love."

7. Oh! What burning flames of holy love does Jesus kindle in the souls who receive Him in this sacrament with a desire of being inflamed with His love. St. Catherine of Sienna saw, one day, in the hands of a priest, Jesus, in the Holy Sacrament, like a furnace of love; and wondered that the hearts of all men were not set on fire and reduced to ashes by the flames which issued from the Holy Eucharist. St. Rose of Lima used to say that, in receiving Jesus Christ, she felt that as if she received the sun. Hence she sent forth from her countenance rays which dazzled the sight, and the heat emitted from her mouth after Communion was so intense, that the person who reached her a drink felt her hand scorched as if she approached a furnace. In visiting the Most Holy Sacrament, St. Wenceslaus, king and martyr, was inflamed, even externally, with such a degree of heat

that the servant who accompanied him, when obliged to walk on the snow, trod in the footsteps of the saint, and thus felt no cold. The Eucharist is a fire which inflames us, that, like lions breathing fire, we may retire from the altar being made terrible to the devil. The Holy Sacrament is a fire which inflames the soul to such a degree that we ought to depart from the altar breathing such flames of love that the devil will no longer dare to tempt us.

8. Jesus has left Himself in the Most Holy Sacrament that all who wish may be able to find Him. On the night on which the Redeemer took leave of His disciples to go to His death, they shed tears of sorrow at the thought of being separated from their dear Master; but Jesus consoled them, saying (and the same He then said to us also), "My children, I am going to die for you, in order to show you the love which I bear you. But at My death I will not leave you alone; as long as you are on earth, I will remain with you in the Most Holy Sacrament. I leave you My body, My soul, My divinity: I leave Myself entirely to you. As long as you remain on earth, I will not depart from you." The Saviour did not wish to leave His spouse alone at such a distance and therefore He has left this sacrament, in which He Himself, the best of all companions, has remained with her. The Gentiles invented so many gods; but they could never have imagined a god more loving than our God, Who remains so near to us, and assists us with so much love. Behold, then, Jesus Christ remains in our tabernacles as if confined in so many prisons of love. His priests remove Him from the tabernacle to expose Him on the altar, or to give Communion, and afterward put Him back to be again

shut up; and Jesus is content to remain there day and night. It would be enough for Him to remain there during the day. But no, He wished to remain also during the night, though left alone, that, in the morning, all who seek Him might instantly find Him. There is not a town nor a convent in which the Holy Sacrament is not kept; and in all these places the King of Heaven is content to remain shut up in a case of wood or of stone, often even without a lamp burning before Him, and without anyone to keep Him company. But, "O Lord!" says St Bernard, "this is not suited to Your Majesty." "No matter," Jesus replies; "if it becomes not My Majesty, it well becomes My love."

9. Jesus Christ, in the Blessed Sacrament, gives audience to all. St. Teresa used to say that all cannot speak with their sovereign or president. The poor can scarcely hope to address him, and make known to him their necessities, even through a third person. But to speak to the King of Heaven, the intervention of a third person is not necessary: all, the poor as well as the nobles of the earth, may speak to Him face to face in the Holy Sacrament. Hence Jesus is called the flower of the fields. The flowers of gardens are enclosed and reserved; but the flowers of the fields are exposed to all. Jesus desires that we speak to Him with unbounded confidence: it is for this purpose that He remains under the species of bread. If Jesus appeared on our altars, as He will on the day of judgement, on a throne of glory, who among would dare to approach Him? But because the Lord desires that we speak to Him and ask His graces with confidence and without fear, He has therefore clothed His majesty with the appearance of bread. He desires that we converse with Him as one friend does with another.

10. Jesus Christ complained to the servant of God, Sr. Margaret Mary Alacoque, of the ingratitude of men to Him in this sacrament of love. To make her understand the love with which He dwells on our altars, He showed her His heart in a throne of flames, surrounded with thorns and surmounted by a cross, and said to her, "Behold the heart, which has loved men so tenderly, which has reserved nothing, and which has been even consumed to show its love for them. But, in return, the greater part of mankind treats Me with ingratitude by their irreverence and by their contempt of My love in this sacrament." Christians do not visit Jesus Christ because they do not love Him. They spend entire hours in the company of friends; and they feel tediousness in conversing half an hour with Jesus Christ. To souls enamoured of God, hours spent before Jesus in the Blessed Sacrament appear moments. St. Francis Xavier laboured the whole day for the salvation of souls; and what was his repose at night? It consisted in remaining before the Holy Sacrament. If, my brother, you do not feel this love for Jesus, endeavour at least to visit Him every day: He will certainly inflame your heart. Ah! Happy will you be, if Jesus, by His grace, inflames you with His love. Then you will despise all the goods of this world. "When," says St Francis de Sales, "a house is on fire, all that is within is thrown out through the windows."

GLORY BE TO THE FATHER   Glory be to the Father, and to the Son, and to the Holy Spirit, as it was in the beginning, is now and ever shall be, world without end. Amen.

THE FATIMA PRAYER   O my Jesus, forgive us our sins, save us from the fires of hell, lead all souls to heaven, especially those in most need of Thy mercy.

CONCLUDING PRAYERS   *Upon completing the recitation of the Holy Rosary, the following prayers are customary, but others too may be added according to one's devotion and preference.*

HAIL HOLY QUEEN   Hail Holy Queen, Mother of Mercy, hail our life, our sweetness and our hope. To thee do we cry, poor banished children of Eve, to thee do we send up our sighs, mourning and weeping in this vale of tears. Turn then, most gracious advocate, thine eyes of mercy towards us, and after this, our exile, show unto us the blessed fruit of thy womb, Jesus. O clement, O loving, O sweet Virgin Mary. Pray for us O holy Mother of God, that we may be made worthy of the promises of Christ.

Let Us Pray   O God, Whose only begotten son, by His life, death and resurrection, has purchased for us the rewards of eternal life, grant we beseech You, that meditating on these mysteries of the most Holy Rosary of the Blessed Virgin Mary, we may both imitate what they contain and obtain what they promise, through the same Christ our Lord. Amen.

PRAYER TO SAINT MICHAEL THE ARCHANGEL   Holy Michael, the Archangel, defend us in the day of battle. Be our safeguard against the wickedness and snares of the devil. May God rebuke him, we humbly pray; and do thou, O Prince of the heavenly hosts, by the power of God thrust down into hell Satan and all the evil spirits who wander through the world seeking the ruin of souls. Amen.

MEMORARE   Remember, O most gracious Virgin Mary, that never was it known that anyone who fled to thy protection, implored thy help, or sought thine intercession was left unaided. Inspired by this confidence, I fly unto thee, O Virgin of virgins, my mother; to thee do I come, before you I stand, sinful and sorrowful. O Mother of the Word Incarnate, despise not my petitions, but in thy mercy hear and answer me. Amen.

May the Divine Assistance remain always with us, and may the souls of the faithful departed, through the mercy of God rest in peace. Amen.

The Hopeful Mysteries

The Creation of all things in Christ

FRUIT OF THIS MYSTERY

Awe of God's plan, decreed from eternity

HE GREAT NAME OF Jesus was not given by man, but by God Himself; "The name of Jesus," says St. Bernard, "was first preordained by God." It was a new name, "A new Name, which the mouth of the Lord shall name." A new name, which God alone could give to Him Whom He destined to be the Saviour of the world. A new and an eternal name; because, as our salvation was decreed from all eternity, so from all eternity was this name given to the Redeemer. He commands that this name should be adored by the angels, by men, and by devils, "That in the Name of Jesus every knee should bow of those that are in heaven, on earth, and under the earth." If, then, all creatures are to adore this great name, still more ought we sinners to adore it, since it was in our behalf that this name of Jesus, which signifies Saviour, was given to Him; and for this end also He came down from heaven, namely, to save sinners.

OUR FATHER   Our Father, Who art in Heaven, hallowed be Thy name, Thy kingdom come, Thy will be done, on earth as it is in heaven. Give us this day our daily bread; and forgive us our trespasses, as we forgive those who trespass against us; and lead us not into temptation, but deliver us from evil. Amen.

HAIL MARY (10)   Hail Mary, Full of Grace, the Lord is with thee. Blessed art thou among women and blessed is the fruit of thy womb, Jesus. Holy Mary, Mother of God, pray for us sinners now, and at the hour of our death. Amen.

1. Who is of higher nobility than God? Illustrious people are proud of the fact that their nobility goes back five hundred or a thousand years; the nobility of God is from all eternity. Who is greater than God? He is the Lord of all. The angels of Heaven and the powerful on earth are to Him as a drop in the mighty ocean or as a miserable grain of dust. A single word from Him brought the world into being; a single word could consign everything to oblivion. Who is richer than God? He possesses the treasures of Heaven and earth. Who is more beautiful than God? The beauty of all

creatures vanishes before the glory of God. Who is more beneficent than God? The efforts of God to bestow favours on us are greater even than our desire to receive them. Who is more merciful than God? As soon as a sinner, though it be the most abandoned wretch on earth, humbles himself before God and repents of his sins, God pardons him and receives him back. Who is more grateful than God? He never permits anything we do for love of Him to go unrewarded. In fine, Who is more amiable and deserving of love than God? His very face fills the saints of Heaven with a delight that constitutes their perfect happiness for all eternity.

2. After God had created the earth He created two lights, the greater and the less: the sun to give light by day, and the moon to give light by night. The sun was the type of Jesus Christ, in Whose light the just rejoice who live in the daylight of divine grace; but the moon was the type of Mary, by whom sinners are enlightened, who are living in the night of sin. Mary, then, being the moon is so propitious to miserable sinners. If any unhappy person finds that he has fallen into this night of sin, what must he do? Since he has lost the light of the sun, by loosing divine grace, let him turn to the moon, let him pray to Mary, and she will give him light to know the misery of his condition, and strength to come forth from it. By the prayers of Mary innumerable sinners are continually converted.

3. The Lord created Adam, who was the first man, and gave him Eve for his wife, that from them mankind might be populated. He created them in His grace, and placed them in the terrestrial paradise, with the promise that they should be

thence transferred to heaven to enjoy complete and eternal felicity. During their sojourn on this earth He gave them for their food all the fruits of that garden of delights; but, to try their obedience, He forbade them to eat the fruit of only one tree, which He pointed out to them.

4. As Almighty God knew that man is won by kindness, He determined to lavish His gifts upon him, and so take captive the affections of his heart. For this reason He said, "I will draw them with the cords of Adam, with the bands of love." I will catch men by those very snares by which they are naturally caught, that is, by the snares of love. And such exactly are all the favours of God to man. After having given him a soul created in His own image, with memory, understanding, and will, and a body with its senses, He created heaven and earth for him, yes, all that exists, all for the love of man; the firmament, the stars, the planets, the seas, the rivers, the fountains, the hills, the plains, metals, fruits, and a countless variety of animals: and all these creatures that they might minister to the uses of man, and that man might love Him in gratitude for so many admirable gifts.

5. Heaven and earth, and all things, tell me to love You, My Lord, whatever I behold on the earth, or above the earth, all speak to me, and exhort me to love You; because all assure me that You have made them for the love of me. The founder of the Trappist order, when from his hermitage he stood and surveyed the hills, the fountains, the birds, the flowers, the planets, and the skies, felt himself animated by each one of these creatures to love that God Who had created all through love of him. In like manner St. Mary

Magdalene of Pazzi, when she held any beautiful flower in her hand, was enkindled by the sight of it with love to God; and she would say, "And God, then, has thought from all eternity of creating this flower for love of me!" Thus did that flower become, as it were, a dart of love, which sweetly wounded her, and united her more and more to her God. On the other hand, St. Teresa, at the sight of trees, fountains, rivers, lakes, or meadows, declared that all these fair things upbraided her for her ingratitude in loving so coldly a God who created them that He might be loved by her. To the like purpose is it related of a pious hermit, that when walking through the country, it seemed to him that the plants and flowers in his path reproached him for the cold return of love he made to God; so that he went along gently striking them with his staff, and saying to them, "Oh, be silent, be silent; you call me an ungrateful wretch; you tell me God has made you for love of me, and yet I do not love Him; but now I understand you, be silent, be silent; do not reproach me any more."

6. God deserves your love, because He has loved you before you loved Him, and because He has been the first of all to love you. Your parents have been the first to love you on this earth; but they have loved you only after they have known you. Before your father or your mother came into this world, God loved you: even before the world was created, He loved you. And how long before the creation of the world did God love you? Perhaps a thousand years, or a thousand ages? It is useless to count years of ages; God has loved you from eternity. In a word, as long as He has been God, He has loved you; as long as He has loved Himself, He

has loved you. Hence the holy virgin St. Agnes had reason
to say, "I am prevented by another lover." When the world
and creatures sought her love, she answered, "No, I cannot
love you. My God has been the first to love me; it is but just,
then, that I should consecrate all my love to Him alone."

7. Consider, moreover, the special love God has shown
to you in allowing you to be born in a Christian country,
and in the bosom of the true Church. How many are born
among idolaters, Jews, Mohammedans, or heretics, and are
all lost! The number of those who have the happiness of
being born in a family where the true faith prevails is small,
compared with the rest of mankind; and He has chosen you
to be one of that small number. Oh, what an infinite gift
is the gift of faith! How many millions are deprived of the
sacraments, of sermon, of the examples of good companions
and of all the other helps to salvation which are found in
the true Church! And God is resolved to give all these great
helps to you without any merit on your part, and even with
a foreknowledge of your demerits; for when He thought
of creating you, and bestowing these graces upon you, He
foresaw the insults with you would offer to Him.

8. My God and my All, I prefer You to all riches, to hon-
ors, to knowledge, to glory, to expectations and to all the
gifts which You could bestow on me. You are entirely my
Good; You alone I desire and nothing more, for You alone
are infinitely beautiful, infinitely kind, infinitely amiable;
in a word, You are the Only Good. Wherefore, every gift
which is not Yourself is not enough for me. I repeat, and
I will ever repeat it, You alone I desire and nothing more;

and whatever is less than You, I tell You, it is not sufficient for me. Oh, when shall it be given me to occupy myself solely in praising You, loving You and pleasing You, so that I shall no more think of creatures, nor even of myself? O men, let us undeceive ourselves! All the good which comes to us from creatures is but dust, smoke and deceits; God alone is He who can satisfy us. But in this life He does not grant us to enjoy Him fully; He only gives us certain foretastes of the good things which He promises in Heaven. There He awaits us to satiate us with His own bliss, when He will say to us, "Enter You into the joy of Your Lord." The Lord gives heavenly consolations to His servants, only to make them yearn for that happiness which He prepares for them in Paradise.

9. We have not been created for this earth; we have been created for the blessed kingdom of Paradise. For this reason it is, says St. Augustine, that God mingles so much bitterness with the delights of the world in order that we may not forget Him and eternal life. If, living as we do amid so many thorns in this life, we are still strongly attached to it, and long so little after Paradise, how necessary, then, is occasional bitterness, to remind us that we are made for God and not merely the pleasures of this earth.

10. Thus we see that the desire to go and see God in heaven, not so much for the delight which we shall experience in loving God, as for the pleasure which we shall afford God by loving Him, is pure and perfect love. Nor is the joy of the blessed in heaven any hindrance to the purity of their of their love; such joy is inseparable from their love; but

they take far more satisfaction in their love of God than in the joy that it affords them. The rewards given by man are distinct from their own persons and independent of them, since they do not bestow themselves, but only their goods, when they give to others. With God however, the principal reward which He gives to the blessed is the gift of Himself, "I am Your reward exceeding great." Hence to desire heaven is the same thing as to desire God, Who is our last end.

GLORY BE TO THE FATHER   Glory be to the Father, and to the Son, and to the Holy Spirit, as it was in the beginning, is now and ever shall be, world without end. Amen.

THE FATIMA PRAYER   O my Jesus, forgive us our sins, save us from the fires of hell, lead all souls to heaven, especially those in most need of Thy mercy.

The Promise of the Redeemer and Co-Redemptrix

THE FRUIT OF THIS MYSTERY

Gratitude to God for His ineffable patience with humanity

ONSIDER THAT GOD ALLOWED thousands of years to pass after the transgression of Adam, before He sent His son upon earth to redeem the world. And in the mean time, oh, what fatal darkness reigned upon the earth! The true God was not known or adored, except in one small corner of the world. Idolatry reigned everywhere;

so that devils and beasts and stones were adored as gods. But let admire in this the Divine Wisdom: He deferred the coming of the Redeemer in order to render His advent more welcome to man, in order that the malice of sin might be better known, as well as the necessity of a remedy and the grace of the Saviour. If Jesus Christ had come into the world immediately after the fall of Adam, the greatness of this favour would have been but slightly appreciated. Let us therefore thank the goodness of God for having sent us into the world after the great work of redemption was accomplished.

OUR FATHER   Our Father, Who art in Heaven, hallowed be Thy name, Thy kingdom come, Thy will be done, on earth as it is in heaven. Give us this day our daily bread; and forgive us our trespasses, as we forgive those who trespass against us; and lead us not into temptation, but deliver us from evil. Amen.

HAIL MARY (10)   Hail Mary, Full of Grace, the Lord is with thee. Blessed art thou among women and blessed is the fruit of thy womb, Jesus. Holy Mary, Mother of God, pray for us sinners now, and at the hour of our death. Amen.

1. After Our Lord had commanded our first parents not to eat of the forbidden fruit, unhappy Eve approached the tree and was addressed from it by the serpent, who said to her, "Why has God forbidden you to eat of this delightful fruit?" Eve replied, "God has commanded us that we should not eat and that we should not touch it, lest perhaps we die." Behold the weakness of Eve! The Lord had absolutely

threatened them with death and she now begins to speak of it as doubtful, "lest perhaps we die." But, the devil seeing that Eve was little in fear of the divine threat, proceeded to encourage her by saying, "No, you shall not die the death;" and thus he deceived her and caused her to waver and to eat the apple. Thus, even now, does the enemy continue to deceive so many poor sinners. God threatens, "Stop and do penance, because otherwise you shall damn yourselves, as so many others have done." The devil says to them, "Fear nothing, sin on, continue to enjoy yourselves, because God is merciful; He will pardon you by and by and you shall be saved." Thus many are deceived, and lose their salvation.

2. As the Blessed Virgin is the mother of love and of hope, thus, also, is she the mother of faith, since Mary, by her faith, repaired that loss which Eve caused by her incredulity. Eve, because she chose to believe the serpent rather than the Word of God, brought death into the world, but our queen, believing the words of the angel, that she, remaining a virgin, was to become the mother of the Lord, brought salvation to the world.

3. God was not satisfied with giving us so many beautiful creatures. He has gone to such lengths to gain our love, as to give Himself to us. The Eternal Father did not hesitate to give us even His only begotten Son. When the Eternal Father saw that we were all dead, and deprived of His grace by sin, what did He do? For the immense love He bore us, He sent His beloved Son to make atonement for us; and so to restore to us that life which sin had robbed us of. He has granted us every good together with Him; His

grace, His love, and Paradise, since assuredly all these gifts are much less than that of His Son. Let us, therefore, love Jesus Christ as much as possible here below. Unfortunately, we miserable children of Adam, infected as we are with sin, cannot love God without some imperfection. It is in heaven alone, where we shall see God face to face, that we shall love Him, nay more, that we shall be necessitated to love Him with all our strength.

4. If Eve had not looked at the forbidden apple, she should not have fallen; but because she saw that it was good to eat, and fair to the eyes, and beautiful to behold, she took of the fruit and ate. The devil first tempts us to look, then to desire, and afterwards to consent. Almost all our rebellious passions spring from unguarded looks; for, generally speaking, it is by the sight that all inordinate affections and desires are excited. Hence, to avoid the sight of dangerous objects, the saints were accustomed to keep their eyes almost continually fixed on the earth, and to abstain even from looking at innocent objects. The indulgence of the eyes, if not productive of any other evil, at least destroys recollection during the time of prayer. Hence it is her duty to abstain from all looks of curiosity, which distract her mind from holy thoughts. Let her eyes be directed only to objects which raise the soul to God.

5. Adam and Eve disobeyed God, and ate the forbidden fruit, and for this sin they were deprived of divine grace, were instantly banished from paradise, and, as rebels to the Divine Majesty, were, with all their posterity, condemned to temporal and eternal death. Thus was heaven shut against

them and all their descendants. This is the Original Sin in which, as children of a rebellious father, we are all born children of wrath and enemies of God. When a vassal rebels against his sovereign, all the descendants of the rebel become hateful to the prince, and are banished from the kingdom. Thus Original Sin, by the disobedience of Adam, deprives us of the grace of God. All are born with the infection of the sin of Adam, in consequence of which we have our understanding darkened to the knowledge of eternal truth and our will inclined towards evil. But by the merits of Jesus Christ at baptism we obtain the divine grace and the remedy for all our misery. We thus become the adopted sons of God and heirs of paradise, provided we preserve till death the grace given to us in baptism. But if we lose it by mortal sin we shall be condemned to Hell, and can only obtain pardon by the sacrament of confession.

6. Noah's ark also prefigured Mary; because as in the ark all animals found refuge, so under the mantle of Mary all sinners find protection, who have made themselves like the beasts by their vices and sensuality. With this difference, the beasts that entered into the ark remained still wild animals; the wolf remained a wolf, the tiger a tiger. But under the mantle of Mary the wolf becomes a lamb, the tiger a dove. St. Gertrude once saw Mary with her mantle outspread, and under it wild beasts of various kinds, leopards, lions, and bears; and the Virgin not only did not drive them from her but with her gentle hand kindly received them and caressed them. The saint understood that these wild beasts were miserable sinners who when they take refuge with Mary are received by her with sweetness and love.

7. Again, Mary was prefigured by Noah's dove, who returned to the ark bearing in its beak the olive-branch, as a sign of the peace which God granted to men. Mary, then, was the heavenly dove who brought to the lost world the olive-branch, a sign of mercy; for she gave us Jesus Christ, Who is the fountain of mercy, and thus obtained, by the price of His merits, all the graces which God gives us. And as through Mary the world received celestial peace, so by means of Mary sinners are constantly becoming reconciled to God. Our Lady could say of herself, "I am that dove of Noah, who brought to the Church universal peace."

8. As a man and a woman have co-operated for our ruin, so it was fit that another man and another woman should co-operate for our restoration; and these were Jesus and His mother Mary. Doubtless, Jesus Christ alone was all-sufficient for our redemption: yet it was more fitting that each sex should take part in our redemption, when both took part in our corruption. For this reason Mary is justly called the co-operatrix with Christ in our redemption: And she herself revealed to St. Bridget, that as Adam and Eve sold the world for one apple, so her son and herself with one heart redeemed the world. God could, indeed, create the world from nothing; but when it was lost by sin, He would not redeem it without the co-operation of Mary.

9. At first the serpent tempted Eve not to eat, but only to behold the forbidden fruit; he then raised doubts about the fulfilment of the divine threats; and in the end induced her to violate the command of God. The enemy is satisfied when a soul begins to open to him the gate of her heart, he

will afterwards obtain full possession of it. The devil does not contend at once against any one by temptations to great vices, but only to small faults, that he may by some means enter and govern the heart of man, and that he may afterwards impel him to more heinous crimes. He does not immediately tempt any one to mortal sin; but commences by suggesting light defects, that, gaining admission into the soul, and beginning his rule, he may afterwards draw her into grievous transgressions. No one, is plunged at once into the depths of depravity, they who fall into the greatest enormities begin by the smallest faults.

10. This earth is the place for meriting, and therefore it is a place for suffering. Our true country, where God has prepared for us repose in everlasting joy, is paradise. We have but a short time to stay in this world; but in this short time we have many labours to undergo. We must suffer, and all must suffer; be they just, or be they sinners, each one must carry his cross. He that carries it with patience is saved; he that carries it with impatience is lost. St. Augustine says, the same miseries send some to Paradise and some to Hell, "One and the same blow lifts the good to glory, and reduces the bad to ashes." By the test of suffering the chaff in the Church of God is distinguished from the wheat: he that humbles himself under tribulations, and is resigned to the will of God, is wheat for Paradise; he that grows haughty and is enraged, and so forsakes God, is chaff for Hell.

GLORY BE TO THE FATHER   Glory be to the Father, and to the Son, and to the Holy Spirit, as it was in the beginning, is now and ever shall be, world without end. Amen.

THE FATIMA PRAYER   O my Jesus, forgive us our sins, save us from the fires of hell, lead all souls to heaven, especially those in most need of Thy mercy.

The Birth of the Immaculate Virgin Mary to Sts. Joachim and Ann

W E SHOULD THEREFORE HOLD it for certain, that the Incarnate Word selected for Himself a befitting mother, and one of whom He need not be ashamed. Jesus felt it no reproach to hear Himself called by the Jews the Son of Mary. But on the other hand, it would doubtless have been a reproach to Him if it could have been said by the demons, "Was He not born from a mother who was a sinner, and once our slave?" It would be considered most unfit that Jesus Christ should have been born of a woman deformed and maimed in body, or possessed by evil spirits; but how much more unseemly that He should be born of a woman once deformed in soul, and possessed by Lucifer. Ah, that God Who is wisdom itself well knew how to prepare upon the earth a fit dwelling for Him to inhabit, "Wisdom has built herself a house." "The Most High has sanctified His own tabernacle." How can we think that the Son of God would have chosen to inhabit the soul and body of Mary without first sanctifying her and preserving her from every stain of sin? The Church sings, "Oh Lord, You did not shrink from the Virgin's womb." Indeed, God would have shrunk from incarnating Himself in the womb of an Agnes, of a Gertrude, of a Theresa, since those virgins, although holy, were for a time, stained with Original Sin; but He did not shrink from becoming man in the womb of Mary, because this chosen Virgin was always pure from every guilt, and never possessed by the infernal serpent. Hence St. Augustine wrote, "The Son of God has built Himself no house more worthy than Mary, who was never taken by the enemy, nor robbed of her ornaments." Who has ever heard of an architect building a house for his own use and then giving the first possession of it to his greatest enemy?

OUR FATHER   Our Father, Who art in Heaven, hallowed be Thy name, Thy kingdom come, Thy will be done, on earth as it is in heaven. Give us this day our daily bread; and forgive us our trespasses, as we forgive those who trespass against us; and lead us not into temptation, but deliver us from evil. Amen.

HAIL MARY (10)   Hail Mary, Full of Grace, the Lord is with thee. Blessed art thou among women and blessed is the fruit of thy womb, Jesus. Holy Mary, Mother of God, pray for us sinners now, and at the hour of our death. Amen.

1. The ruin was great which accursed sin brought upon Adam and the whole human race; for when he unhappily lost grace, he at the same time drew upon himself, and upon all his descendants, both the displeasure of God, and all other evils. But God ordained that the blessed Virgin should be exempt from this common calamity, for He had destined her to be the mother of the Second Adam, Jesus Christ, Who was to repair the injury done by the first.

2. it was fitting that God should preserve her from Original Sin, since He destined her to bruise the head of the infernal serpent, who, by seducing our first parents, brought death upon all men. Now, if Mary was to be the strong woman brought into the world to crush Lucifer, surely it was not fitting that she should first be conquered by Lucifer, and made his slave, but rather that she should be free from every stain, and from all subjection to the enemy. As he had in his pride already corrupted the whole human race, he would also corrupt the pure soul of this virgin. But may the divine goodness be ever praised, Who prevented her with so much grace, to the end that remaining free from every stain of sin, she could overthrow and confound his pride. As the devil was the head from whence Original Sin proceeded,

that head Mary crushed, because no sin ever entered the soul of the Virgin, and therefore she was free from all stain.

3. Oh, how the devils tremble, exclaims St. Bernard, if they only hear the name of Mary uttered! As men fall to the earth through fear, when a thunderbolt strikes near them, so the devils fall prostrate when but the name of Mary is heard. How many noble victories have the servants of Mary not gained over these enemies by the power of her most holy name! Many persons, at the mention of the name of Mary have been delivered from great dangers. Very glorious, oh Mary, and wonderful, is your great name. Those who are mindful to utter it at the hour of death, have nothing to fear from hell, for the devils at once abandon the soul when they hear the name of Mary. Oh, if Christians were mindful in temptations to invoke with confidence the name of Mary, it is certain that they would never fall.

4. Men are accustomed to celebrate the birth of their children with joy and feasting; but rather they ought to weep and give signs of grief and mourning, considering that these are born, not only destitute of merits and of reason, but moreover infected by sin and children of wrath, and therefore condemned to misery and death. But with reason do we celebrate, with feasts and universal praise, the birth of our infant Mary, for she came into this world an infant in age, it is true, but great in merits and in virtue. Mary was born a saint, and a great saint.

5. Our heavenly child, because she was appointed mediatrix of the world, as well as predestined to be the mother of the

Redeemer, even from the first moment of her life, received greater grace than that of all the saints united. Hence how lovely in the sight of heaven and earth was the beautiful soul of that happy infant, although still enclosed in the womb of its mother! In the eye of God she was the creature most worthy of love, because, already full of grace and of merit, she could, even at that time, exult and say, "When I was a little child I pleased the Most High." And at the same time she was the creature most full of love for God that until that time had appeared in this world; so that Mary, had she been born immediately after her most pure conception, would have come into the world more rich in merits, and more holy, than all the saints united.

6. It is the opinion of the whole world, that the holy infant, when she received sanctifying grace in the womb of St. Ann, received at the same time the perfect use of reason, with a great divine light corresponding to the grace with which she was enriched. Hence we may believe, that from the first moment when her pure soul was united to her most pure body, she was enlightened with divine wisdom to comprehend eternal truths, the beauty of virtue, above all, the infinite goodness of her God, and how much He deserves to be loved by all men, but especially by her, on account of the peculiar graces with which He had adorned her and distinguished her from all creatures; preserving her from the stain of original sin and destining her to be the mother of the Word and the queen of the universe.

7. From the moment of her conception Mary loved God with all her strength, and thus continued to love Him

through all those nine months that she lived before her birth. She was free from Original Sin, and therefore she was also exempt from every earthly attachment, from every irregular tendency, from every distraction, from all strife of the senses, which could have prevented her from advancing constantly in the divine love. All her senses united with her blessed spirit in drawing her near to God. Hence her pure soul, freed from every hindrance, without lingering, always rose to God, always loved Him, and always increased in love to Him. Therefore, she described herself to a saint as "a tree planted by the waters".

8. Let us rejoice, then, with our infant, who was born so holy, so dear to God, and so full of grace; and let us rejoice not only for her, but also for ourselves, since she came into the world full of grace, not only for her own glory, but for our good. Hence what St. John said of Jesus, "And of His fullness we all have received" the saints say of Mary. There is no one who does not share in the grace of Mary, for is there any one in the world to whom Mary is not merciful, and on whom she does not bestow some favour? From Jesus we receive grace as from the author of grace, from Mary as the advocate; from Jesus as the fountain, from Mary as the channel.

9. God has established Mary as the channel of the mercies which He wishes to dispense to men; and for this reason He filled her with grace, that every one might receive his portion of her fullness. Miserable is that soul who closes for herself this channel of grace, by neglecting to recommend herself to Mary! When Holofernes wished to make himself

master of the city of Bethulia, he ordered the aqueducts to be destroyed. And this the devil does when he wishes to make himself master of a soul, he makes her abandon the devotion to the most holy Mary. What ruin a man brings upon himself if he closes this channel, and abandons devotion to this queen of heaven.

10. The Blessed Virgin, not being able fully to thank the Lord for all the favours bestowed on her, is pleased when her children help her to thank God. We can do this by reverencing the saints who are most closely united to Mary, that is, St. Joseph, St. Joachim, St. Ann, St. John the Baptist and St. John the Evangelist. The Virgin herself recommended to a nobleman the devotion to St. Ann her mother. Resolve to preach, or at least recommend to all, particularly to one's relatives, devotion to the divine mother and her holy relations. That, as we commemorate them, they may deign to intercede for us.

GLORY BE TO THE FATHER   Glory be to the Father, and to the Son, and to the Holy Spirit, as it was in the beginning, is now and ever shall be, world without end. Amen.

THE FATIMA PRAYER   O my Jesus, forgive us our sins, save us from the fires of hell, lead all souls to heaven, especially those in most need of Thy mercy.

The Presentation of Mary in the Temple as a Girl

THE FRUIT OF THIS MYSTERY

Nearness to God in one's daily duties

"RISE, MAKE HASTE, MY love, my dove, my beautiful one, and come!" Mary well understood the voice of God calling her to devote herself to His love. And thus enlightened she at once offered herself to her Lord. Behold, O Mary, I this day present myself to you, and in union with you I renounce all creatures and devote myself entirely to the love of my Creator.

OUR FATHER   Our Father, Who art in Heaven, hallowed be Thy name, Thy kingdom come, Thy will be done, on earth as it is in heaven. Give us this day our daily bread; and forgive us our trespasses, as we forgive those who trespass against us; and lead us not into temptation, but deliver us from evil. Amen.

HAIL MARY (10)   Hail Mary, Full of Grace, the Lord is with thee. Blessed art thou among women and blessed is the fruit of thy womb, Jesus. Holy Mary, Mother of God, pray for us sinners now, and at the hour of our death. Amen.

1. What soul was ever more detached from the things of the world, and more united to God, than the beautiful soul of Mary? She was indeed entirely detached from her parents, since at the age of three years, when children are most dependent on their parents, and have the greatest need of their assistance, Mary with so great resolution left them, and went to shut herself up in the Temple to attend to the things of God. She was detached from riches, contented to live always poor, and supporting herself with the labour of her hands. She was detached from honours, loving a humble and abject life, although queenly honour belonged to her, for she traced her descent from the kings of Israel. The Virgin herself revealed to a saint, that when she was left in the temple by her parents, she resolved in her heart to have no other father, and to love no other good but God.

2. "Hearken, O daughter, and see, and incline your ear; and forget your people and your father's house." The holy Virgin obeyed the divine call with promptitude and with generosity. From the first moment that the heavenly child was sanctified in her mother's womb, which was at the instant of her Immaculate Conception, she received the perfect use of reason and she began to merit. And immediately, as an angel revealed to St. Bridget, our Queen determined to sacrifice her will to God, and to give Him all her love for the whole of her life.

3. Mary, hearing that her holy parents, St. Joachim and St. Ann, had consecrated her by vow to God, requested them with earnestness to take her to the Temple, and accomplish their promise. At the age of three years, Mary desired to consecrate herself to God. O beloved Mother of God, most amiable child, Mary, who presented yourself in the Temple, and with promptitude and without reserve did consecrate yourself to the glory and love of God; O that I could offer you this day the first years of my life, to devote myself without reserve to your service, my holy and most sweet Lady! But it is now too late to do this, for I have lost many years in the service of the world. Woe to that time in which I did not love you! But it is better to begin now at least than not at all. O Mary, I this day present myself to you, and in union with you I renounce all creatures and devote myself entirely to the love of my Creator. Help my weakness by your powerful intercession.

4. Behold, then, Joachim and Ann, generously sacrificing to God the most precious treasure they possessed in the

world, and the treasure dearest to their hearts. They set forth from Nazareth carrying their well-beloved little daughter in turn, for she could not otherwise have undertaken so long a journey as that from Nazareth to Jerusalem, a distance of eighty miles. They were accompanied by few relatives, but choirs of angels escorted and served the Immaculate little Virgin, who was about to consecrate herself to the Divine Majesty. "O how beautiful", must the angels have sung, "and how acceptable to God is your every step taken on the way to present and offer yourself to Him, O noble daughter, most beloved of our Lord!"

5. Having reached Jerusalem they brought their cherished little daughter to the Temple. The holy child immediately ascended to the first step, and turning to her parents, on her knees kissed their hands and asked them to bless her and to recommend her to God. After having received the blessing, and being strengthened by the love with which she was going to serve her God, Who had deigned to call her to His house, she ascended all the steps of the Temple. She went up with so much haste and zeal that she turned back no more, not even to look on her parents who remained there deeply afflicted, and at the same time filled with wonder at the sight of so much strength and courage in so young a child.

6. God Himself with the whole Heavenly Court made great rejoicings on the day that Mary presented herself to be His Spouse in the Temple. For He never saw a holier creature, or one He so tenderly loved, come to offer herself to Him. She bade farewell to the world, and renouncing all the pleasures

it promises to its votaries, she offered and consecrated herself
to her Creator. Many who are sent by God into this world
unfortunately remain to feed on earthly goods. It was not
thus our heavenly dove, Mary, acted. She knew that God
should be our only Good, our only Hope, our only Love;
and she knew that the world is full of dangers, and that he
who leaves it the soonest is most free from its snares. Hence
she sought to do this from her tenderest years, and as soon
as possible shut herself up in the sacred retirement of the
Temple, where she could the better hear God's voice, and
honour and love Him more.

7. Let us consider that this wonderful child, as soon as
she found herself in the Temple, first presented herself to
her mistress, and on her knees humbly besought her to
teach her all that she had to do. Afterwards she saluted her
companions and begged them to condescend to admit her
into their society. After these acts of reverence and humility,
the youthful Mary turned all her thoughts towards God.
She prostrated and kissed the floor for joy of being in the
house of the Lord. She adored His infinite Majesty, and
thanked Him for the great favour she was receiving from
Him, namely, that He had so sweetly arranged for her to
come to live for a time in His house. Then it was that she
offered herself entirely to God, without the least reserve,
by consecrating to Him all her faculties and all her senses,
her whole mind and her whole heart, her whole soul and
her whole body. Again, Mary offered herself thus entirely
without limitation of time; for by this offering of herself she
had the intention of devoting herself to the service of God
in the Temple during her whole life, if such should be the

good pleasure of the Lord, and never to depart from this holy place. "Behold me now before You, O Lord", this holy child must have said, "I come into Your house only to be Your servant; accept the desire I have of rendering You all the honour I can render, and receive me into Your service by giving me grace to be faithful to You."

8. Let us consider how holy and pleasing to God was the life of Mary in the Temple. She progressed without intermission in the perfection of every virtue, as the morning rising. Who can describe how from day to day all her virtues appeared more beautiful, especially her modesty, silence, mortification, humility, sweetness. She was accustomed to speak little, was affable, charitable towards every one, and most obliging. She did not walk, she flew, in the way of the Lord, her blessed soul was the abode of every virtue. She spent a certain time as it is related, in doing some work that had been assigned to her. But the greatest part of the day and of the night she consecrated to prayer and to close communion with God in solitude; for this was the most cherished and most desired occupation of her heart that was burning with love; it was her sweetest delight. Oh, how ardently did Mary in the Temple know how to entreat God for great work of the redemption of the world! Seeing clearly the miserable condition of the world, in which so many souls were lost, in which so few knew the true God, and among this number so few who loved Him. How much better than Patriarchs and Prophets did she pray, "Come, O Lord, do not delay! Show us Your mercy, and send us the Lamb that is to rule the world. You heavens, let your rain

descend and send down the Just, that the earth may bring forth the Saviour."

9. The life of Mary in the temple was but one continual exercise of love, and the offering of her whole self to her Lord. She increased from hour to hour, nay, from moment to moment, in holy virtues, sustained indeed by divine grace, but always endeavouring, with all her powers, to correspond with grace. Mary thus regulated her life: In the morning until the third hour she remained in prayer; from the third hour until the ninth she employed herself with work; and from the ninth hour she again prayed until the Angel brought her food, as he was accustomed to do. She was always the first in vigils, the most exact in the observance of the divine law, the most profoundly humble, and the most perfect in every virtue. No one ever saw her angry, her every word carried such sweetness with it that it was a witness to all that God was with her.

10. Thus Mary, a young virgin in the temple, devoted herself to prayer. And seeing the human race lost and hateful to God, she especially prayed for the coming of the Messiah, desiring then to be the servant of that happy Virgin who was to be the mother of God. The love of this exalted child hastened the coming of the redeemer into the world. And whilst she, in her humility, looked upon herself as unworthy to be the servant of the Divine Mother, she was herself chosen to be this mother; and by the sweet odour of her virtues and her powerful prayers she drew the Divine Son into her virginal womb. For this reason Mary was called a turtle-dove by her Divine Spouse, not only because as a

turtle-dove she always loved solitude, living in this world as in a desert, but also because, like a turtle-dove, which always sighs for its companions, Mary always sighed in the temple, compassionating the miseries of the lost world, and seeking from God the redemption of all.

GLORY BE TO THE FATHER   Glory be to the Father, and to the Son, and to the Holy Spirit, as it was in the beginning, is now and ever shall be, world without end. Amen.

THE FATIMA PRAYER   O my Jesus, forgive us our sins, save us from the fires of hell, lead all souls to heaven, especially those in most need of Thy mercy.

The Chaste Espousals of Mary and Joseph

THE FRUIT OF THIS MYSTERY

Admiration of St. Joseph, the chaste spouse of Our Lady

JOSEPH WAS HOLY BEFORE his marriage, but still more so after his union with the divine mother; the bare example of his holy spouse would have been sufficient to sanctify him. But if Mary, is the dispensatrix of all the graces which God bestows on man, how profusely must she not have enriched her spouse with graces, whom she so much loved, and who loved her so well. How immensely must not the sanctity of Joseph have been increased by the conversation and familiarity of Our Lady during the time they lived together.

OUR FATHER   Our Father, Who art in Heaven, hallowed be Thy name, Thy kingdom come, Thy will be done, on earth as it is in heaven. Give us this day our daily bread; and forgive us our trespasses, as we forgive those who trespass against us; and lead us not into temptation, but deliver us from evil. Amen.

HAIL MARY (10)   Hail Mary, Full of Grace, the Lord is with thee. Blessed art thou among women and blessed is the fruit of thy womb, Jesus. Holy Mary, Mother of God, pray for us sinners now, and at the hour of our death. Amen.

1. From her childhood Mary was filled with the Holy Spirit, and as she advanced in age she advanced also in grace. Thenceforward she determined to love God with her whole heart, so that she might never offend Him, either by her words or actions; and therefore she despised all earthly goods. She gave all she could to the poor. In her food she was so temperate, that she took only as much as was barely necessary to sustain the life of her body.

2. Our most loving Redeemer, that we might learn from Him to despise the things of the world, was pleased to be poor on earth. Behold Mary, His most perfect disciple, who indeed imitated His example. Mary could have lived in comfort on the property she inherited from her parents,

but she preferred to remain poor, and reserving only a small portion for herself, distributed the rest in alms to the Temple and the poor. Many authors are of opinion that Mary even made a vow of poverty; and we know that she herself said to St. Bridget, "From the beginning I vowed in my own heart that I would never possess anything on earth." Out of love for poverty she did not disdain to marry St. Joseph, who was only a poor carpenter, and afterwards to maintain herself by the work of her hands, spinning and sewing. The Angel, speaking of Mary, told St. Bridget that "worldly riches were of no more value in her eyes than mire." In a word, she lived always poor, and she died poor; for at her death we know that she only possessed two poor gowns; which she left to the two virgins who had served her during her life.

3. The beauty of Mary surpassed the beauty of all men and angels. She was most beautiful, I repeat, but without injury to those who looked upon her, for her beauty put to flight impure emotions, and suggested even pure thoughts. So great grace had she, that she not only preserved her own virginity, but also conferred a remarkable gift of purity on those who beheld her. Therefore she was called 'myrrh', which prevents corruption. She was occupied in active life, but labour did not interrupt her union with God. In the contemplative life she was recollected in God, but without neglect of the temporal life, and of the charity due to her neighbour.

4. On discovering in the Sacred Scriptures that God was to be born of a virgin, that He might redeem the world, her soul was to such a degree inflamed with divine love, that

she could desire and think of nothing but God; and finding pleasure in Him alone, she avoided all company, even that of her parents, lest their presence might deprive her of His remembrance. She desired, with the greatest ardour, to live until the time of the coming of the Messiah, that she might be the servant of that happy virgin, who merited to be His mother.

5. Consider the love which Joseph bore to his holy spouse. Of all the women who had ever lived, Mary was the most beautiful. She was more humble, more meek, more pure, more obedient, more inflamed with the love of God, than all Angels or all men who have been, or shall be, created. Hence Our Lady merited all the affections of Joseph, who was so great a lover of virtue. Add to this, the tenderness with which he saw himself loved by Mary, who certainly loved her own spouse above all creatures. Besides, Joseph regarded her as the beloved of God, chosen to be the mother of His only-begotten son. Consider how great must have been the affection which, for all these reasons, the just and grateful heart of Joseph entertained for so amiable a spouse as Mary.

6. The fair and pure virgin mother renders all her servants chaste and pure. Even when Mary was on the earth, by her presence she inspired with the love of purity all those who looked upon her. She was called 'the lily among thorns'. All other virgins, are thorns either to themselves or to others; but the blessed Virgin was neither a thorn to herself nor to others, for she inspired with pure and holy affection all those who beheld her. Even the image of this chaste turtle-dove extinguishes the sensual emotions of him who looks upon

it with devotion. Oh, how especially powerful is the name of Mary, in conquering all temptations to vice! Oh Mary, most pure, make my body pure and my soul holy.

7. We should especially be devout to St. Joseph in order that the saint may obtain us a happy death. He, on account of having saved the Infant Jesus from the snares of Herod, has the special privileges of delivering dying persons from the snares of the devil. Moreover, on account of the services he rendered for so many years to Jesus and Mary, having by his labours provided them a dwelling and food, he has the privilege of obtaining the special assistance of Jesus and Mary for his devout clients at death. My holy protector, St. Joseph, on account of my sins I deserve a bad death; but if You defend me I shall not be lost. You were not only a great friend of my Judge, but you were also His guardian and adopted father; recommend me to your Jesus, Who loves you so much. I place myself under your protection; accept me for your perpetual servant. And by that holy company of Jesus and Mary which you did enjoy on earth, obtain that I may never more be separated from their love; and, in fine, by the assistance of Jesus and Mary, which you had at death, obtain for me, that at my death I also may have the special assistance of Jesus and Mary. Most holy Virgin, by the love which you did bear to your holy spouse St. Joseph, help me at the hour of my death.

8. If the two disciples who were going to Emmaus, found themselves influenced with love, in the few moments during which the Saviour walked and conversed with them, so as to say, "Was not our heart burning within us whilst He spoke

with us on the way." What a fire of holy charity must we not believe to have been enkindled in the heart of Joseph by thirty years conversation with Jesus Christ, by hearing constantly from Him the Word of Life, by observing His perfect humility, patience and obedience, by seeing Him so ready to assist Him in his labours in every thing which required to be done about the house? What a conflagration of divine love must not those torches of charity have spread in the breast of Joseph, a breast which was free from every earthly affection. It is true that he had a great love for his spouse Mary; but his was not a divided love. No, the love which he felt for his spouse, filled him still more with divine love, and therefore, we cannot doubt that Joseph whilst he lived with Jesus Christ, increased so much in sanctity and merits, that we may say he excels all the other saints.

9. The apostle writes that Jesus Christ, in the other world, "Will render to every man according to his works." With what glory, do you think, he must have adorned Joseph, who so faithfully loved and served Him on this earth? On the last day, the Saviour will say to His elect, "For I was hungry, and you gave Me to eat; I was thirsty, and you gave Me to drink; I was a stranger, and you took Me in; naked, and you covered Me." Those have fed, and lodged, and clothed Jesus Christ, in the person of the poor; but St. Joseph procured food, and raiment, and lodging, for Jesus Christ in person. Moreover, the Lord has promised a reward to whosoever gives a poor man a drop of cold water in His name. Who can tell what ought to be the reward of Joseph, of him, who can say to Jesus Christ, "Lord, I have not only furnished You with food and raiment, and lodging, but have even

saved You from death, by rescuing You from the sword of Herod." All this should serve to increase our confidence in Joseph, by bringing us to the conclusion, that on account of all these merits, God cannot deny him any favour which he solicits for his clients.

10. It was a delight to the Lord to behold this tender virgin always ascending towards the highest perfection, like a pillar of smoke, rich in the sweet odour of all virtues, as the Holy Spirit Himself clearly describes her in the sacred Canticles, "Who is she that goes up by the desert as a pillar of smoke, of aromatic spices, of myrrh and frankincense, and of all the powers of the perfumer?" Mary was truly God's garden of delights; for He found in her every kind of flower, and all the sweet odours of virtues. God chose Mary for His mother in this world, because He did not find on earth a virgin more holy and more perfect than she was, nor any dwelling more worthy than her most sacred womb.

GLORY BE TO THE FATHER   Glory be to the Father, and to the Son, and to the Holy Spirit, as it was in the beginning, is now and ever shall be, world without end. Amen.

THE FATIMA PRAYER   O my Jesus, forgive us our sins, save us from the fires of hell, lead all souls to heaven, especially those in most need of Thy mercy.

CONCLUDING PRAYERS   *Upon completing the recitation of the Holy Rosary, the following prayers are customary, but others too may be added according to one's devotion and preference.*

HAIL HOLY QUEEN   Hail Holy Queen, Mother of Mercy, hail our life, our sweetness and our hope. To thee do we cry, poor banished children of Eve, to thee do we send up our sighs, mourning and weeping in this vale of tears. Turn then, most gracious advocate, thine eyes of mercy towards us, and after this, our exile, show unto us the blessed fruit of thy womb, Jesus. O clement, O loving, O sweet Virgin Mary. Pray for us O holy Mother of God, that we may be made worthy of the promises of Christ.

Let Us Pray   O God, Whose only begotten son, by His life, death and resurrection, has purchased for us the rewards of eternal life, grant we beseech You, that meditating on these mysteries of the most Holy Rosary of the Blessed Virgin Mary, we may both imitate what they contain and obtain what they promise, through the same Christ our Lord. Amen.

PRAYER TO SAINT MICHAEL THE ARCHANGEL   Holy Michael, the Archangel, defend us in the day of battle. Be our safeguard against the wickedness and snares of the devil. May God rebuke him, we humbly pray; and do thou, O Prince of the heavenly hosts, by the power of God thrust down into hell Satan and all the evil spirits who wander through the world seeking the ruin of souls. Amen.

MEMORARE   Remember, O most gracious Virgin Mary, that never was it known that anyone who fled to thy protection, implored thy help, or sought thine intercession was left unaided. Inspired by this confidence, I fly unto thee, O Virgin of virgins, my mother; to thee do I come, before you I stand, sinful and sorrowful. O Mother of the Word

Incarnate, despise not my petitions, but in thy mercy hear and answer me. Amen.

May the Divine Assistance remain always with us, and may the souls of the faithful departed, through the mercy of God rest in peace. Amen.

Manufactured by Amazon.ca
Acheson, AB